FINDING FITNESS FREEDOM
A Women's Guide to Lifting Weights

NICKI BRIGHT
B.S. Biology
Certified Personal Trainer

Dedicated to my parents,
whose commitment to their own health created a powerful example.

Copyright © 2023 Nicki Bright

All rights reserved. No part of this publication may be reproduced in any form, or by any means, electronic or mechanical, including photocopying, recording, or any information browsing, storage, or retrieval system, without permission in writing from the publisher.

Illustrations copyright © 2023 by Nicki Bright
Cover photograph copyright © 2023 by Michael Scudder

First paperback edition August 2023

ISBN 979-8-3674-8289-8 (paperback)

Published by Nicki Bright
https://nickibright3.wixsite.com/nickiruns

Please be aware that the content contained within this book is not intended to provide medical advice. Rather, it is an account of my personal fitness journey and the knowledge I have acquired as a personal trainer.

It is designed to offer insights, strategies, and anecdotes that may be helpful in your own pursuit of a healthier lifestyle. It is important to consult with a qualified healthcare professional or medical expert for individualized advice pertaining to your specific health needs.

TABLE OF CONTENTS

A Letter to the Reader 1

01 My Story 7

02 A Brief History of Women and Exercise 39

03 Everyone Should Lift Weights 51

04 Work Smarter, Not Harder 61

05 Gym Anxiety 79

06 Establishing Discipline 97

07 The Six Fundamental Exercises 107

08 Workout Programs 135

09 The Basics of Nutrition 151

10 Fad Diets and The Only Diet You Should Be On 173

Main Muscle Groups 189

Glossary of Weightlifting Terms 193

NICKI BRIGHT

A LETTER TO THE READER

Dear Reader,

When you think of a bodybuilder, the image that probably comes to mind is a 300-pound man, aggressively chugging a protein shake with one hand while effortlessly curling a dumbbell with the other. It's an image often associated with the world of bodybuilding. However, it should not be confined to this narrow stereotype. In truth, every single one of us is a bodybuilder.

You see, bodybuilders are people who actively shape their bodies through the choices they make each day—deciding to either elevate and nourish their bodies or to neglect and break them down. What you eat, how you move, and how you care for your body all contribute to the ongoing construction of your physical and emotional self. In this way, bodybuilding is a continuous journey of self-improvement, self-discovery, and self-care, regardless of our goals or aspirations.

By reading this book, you are now on a fitness journey that diverges from the stereotypical notions of strict diets and excessive exercise regimens. Instead, you will discover a refreshing approach to fitness that embraces flexibility, moderation, and self-compassion—a concept I like to call "fitness freedom."

The underlying philosophy of fitness freedom is rooted in the understanding that your health is your true wealth. Just as financial freedom provides the means to afford the lifestyle you desire, fitness freedom empowers you with the knowledge and capacity to achieve any fitness outcome you aspire to.

It's a mindset shift that allows you to break free from the constraints of deprivation and rigid routines and instead encourages a sustainable approach to fitness; one that promotes a balance between your health goals and the enjoyment of life's pleasures.

Throughout most of my formative years, it seemed that everyone else already had found fitness freedom. Meanwhile, I found myself trapped in an unrelenting cycle of self-imposed restrictions, hoping that strict diets or excessive exercise regimens would eventually lead me to the freedom I witnessed in others. I perpetually chided myself for not being more disciplined, the constant disappointment gradually eroding at my self-esteem.

In order to break free from that damaging mindset, I had to get out of my comfort zone and try a new form of exercise, one that at first I met with great hesitation and resistance. Not even two months into this new method of training and I knew I had found the solution I had been looking for my whole life.

Unknowingly stumbling upon fitness freedom, I immediately felt an overwhelming sense of obligation to share my discovery with those who were going through similar struggles. I wanted to tell them: it's not you, your drive, or your work ethic that's holding you back. It's simply a lack of knowledge on how to get there.

The most shocking part about fitness freedom is that it's not as hard to find as you might think. My goal in sharing my story is to illuminate the path to a new way of life—one that is simpler, easier, and breathtakingly liberating.

As a personal trainer, I found myself overflowing with information that I wanted to share with my clients. Yet, despite my sincere efforts, I couldn't shake the nagging feeling that I was falling short in conveying all that I knew in a simplified manner. It became clear that I needed to come up with a more accessible approach. So, I started writing a book.

This book is a meticulously researched and evidence-based guide that will allow you to find fitness freedom. It will serve as your roadmap to navigate through the maze of fad diets, misleading information, persuasive marketing tactics, and outdated perspectives. Moreover, it's an intimate and emotionally charged narrative that recounts my personal journey and transformation, ultimately shaping the person I am today.

This is a call to action—an invitation for you to prioritize your health by honoring your body and nurturing your mind. The time has come for you to take charge of your health and embark on a journey towards a healthier, happier, and more vibrant you.

May this book and my words be your companion. Bring it to the gym with you, keep it cracked open while you shop for groceries, and read it before bed at night. Together, we will navigate through the seas of confusion and uncertainty and emerge on the shores of pure strength and confidence.

Your transformation awaits—let's take the first step together.

Sincerely,

Nicki Bright

NICKI BRIGHT

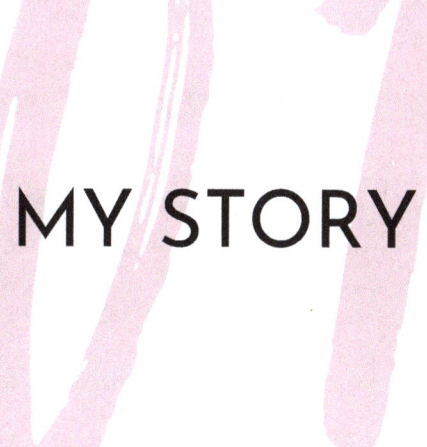

MY STORY

I was raised on adventure.

It all began when my mom, dad, brother, and I packed ourselves like sardines into the family van and embarked on the 16-hour drive to Yellowstone National Park in Wyoming. When we arrived at our destination, I slid open the van door and was welcomed by the fresh smell of pine trees and earth. I stretched my arms out wide with sleep into the crisp air, leaning into the hushed whispers of the forest.

There were many breathtaking sights on that trip, like big-horned moose, exploding geysers, hot springs, and sulfur pools the color of galaxies. We camped throughout the park, playing cards in the tent and swatting at mosquitoes in the late hours of the night. The days were filled with hikes in the mountains, crossing streams, singing songs, and laughing until our sides ached. The nights were filled with warm meals and late talks by a crackling campfire.

2012
Yellowstone National Park, Wyoming

My parents could have taken their kids to a Disneyland resort, like most of my friend's families did. I fantasized about gorging on sweets and lounging by the hotel pool all day. Instead, my brother and I were taught how to pack

FINDING FITNESS FREEDOM

snacks for a long hike and pick the right water shoes for river rafting. These experiences ingrained within me a profound yearning—a genuine hunger—for the great outdoors.

Several months later, I found myself sitting at a desk in elementary school, unable to take my eyes off the cover of my science textbook. In elaborate detail, two people stood on the summit of a mountain, a wide valley below them. Their heavy backpacks and dirty boots told a tale of endurance and resilience. The photograph emanated a palpable sense of accomplishment, sparking a fire of curiosity within me. It was as if the image carried the weight of their triumphant journey, igniting a deep longing to experience my own moments of personal accomplishment.

Every time I looked at that textbook, I wished I had the ability to teleport myself to the top of the mountain to join the hikers. However, reality would always settle back in, once again trapped in a sea of twenty desks filled with children. It was at that time that I realized there was much more learning and discovery waiting for me beyond the four walls of my classroom.

Luckily, my parents took my brother and I on many more family trips to the National Parks, like Joshua Tree, the Grand Canyon, the Sequoias, and Kings Canyon. Despite our annual trips, it felt as if nothing could quench my thirst for the outdoors. Every time we would return from some epic adventure, a bittersweet feeling would wash over me in which I longed to return to those magnificent landscapes and relive those moments.

Throughout my childhood, I was involved in many sports teams. My first endeavor was soccer. Picture me: six years old, sitting in the middle of the field, picking flowers, completely unaware of my surroundings. The ball would sail past me, the other kids aggressively chasing after it. My parents would watch me do this week after week, and it became quickly evident that I wasn't interested in becoming a professional soccer player.

When I was 13, I played on a volleyball team. I spent enough time practicing and refining my skills to improve quickly. My teammates noticed my efforts and were able to rely on me to hit a powerful serve. At the same time, I was involved in the concert band at my school and was quickly improving on the clarinet.

As I approached middle school graduation, the pressing reality of having to make a choice between music or volleyball for my high school elective emerged. Although my heart desperately wanted to continue pursuing both passions, that was not an option. I had to pick one.

With an eagerness to explore my musical talents and forge lasting connections, I decided to join the marching band. The finality of my choice was bittersweet, as I was excited for the year ahead, yet knew I had untapped potential in volleyball—potential that I would never see through.

2014
Playing bass drum in the marching band

Throughout the next several years, I played in the jazz band, concert orchestra, pit orchestra, and drum line. I played many instruments, including the clarinet, xylophone, and bass drum. The friendships forged and the treasured memories created during those two years hold immeasurable value. However, it was during the summer of my sophomore year in high school that a new passion swiftly claimed the top spot in my heart.

FINDING FITNESS FREEDOM

Running was introduced to me through my brother and dad. At ages 13 and 56, they had just completed the 2015 Los Angeles Marathon, a 26.2-mile race beginning at Dodger's Stadium and ending at the Santa Monica Pier. They ran with a group from my brother's middle school called SRLA: Students Run the Los Angeles Marathon. Watching them cross the finish line as I stood from the sidelines, I knew I wanted to be on the course with them next year.

My mom ran the Los Angeles Marathon twice before but didn't plan to run it again due to knee injuries. When she was training, she would always encourage me to run with her. Several times, I remember taking her up on her offer, even though she was much faster than me. Those days, I ran because of my love for her, not for the love for running.

But that all changed one random summer afternoon. I was feeling a surge of inspiration and realizing how rare this was, I seized the opportunity. "Mom, I'm going to run a mile. I'll be back in 10 minutes."

To this day, I remember the joy that lit up her face as soon as I said that. I think there might even have been a tear in her eye.

When I came bursting back into the house, my cheeks were redder than a sunburn and I was dripping with perspiration. My face was flushed, and my hair was sopping wet, but I didn't care about anything. I had one mile under my belt.

The very next day, I laced up my shoes and ran another mile. Every day that week, I ran one mile. A week later, I was ready for the next level: two miles. Several days later, three miles.

I pushed myself further each week, loving the sweat that would soak my clothes and the sound of my shoes pounding the pavement. I loved the wave of accomplishment and pride that would envelop me after each further distance. Within me, a fervent passion for running had ignited.

Before I knew it, the hot summer was over and long school days were back. After a day full of math, chemistry, and English at the high school, I would drive to the middle school and train with my brother's running team. My dad never missed an opportunity to spend time with my brother and I, so he was always there for the afternoon run. Most of the time, the three of us strayed from the group, finding ourselves far ahead, pushing the pace and covering more distance.

The SRLA team ran a "4:1," which meant to run for four minutes and then walk for one. They did this to ensure that all the kids finished the marathon. However, after one run with the team at their pace, I knew I was ready to go much faster.

The 4:1 method was a safe approach, one that would guarantee I finished. But it would also hold me back from running a much faster race—one I knew I was capable of. Knowing this, my dad, brother, and I would abandon the SRLA team after running with them for a couple of miles and push the pace to around 8:30 to 10 minutes per mile. Although no one had said it out loud, we all knew we were training to run a marathon in under four hours.

Many months of intense training later, we found ourselves standing in the dark parking lot of Dodger's Stadium at 4:30 a.m. We were at the start line for the 2016 Los Angeles Marathon, and it was February 14, Valentine's Day.

Above us, the night sky transformed gradually, evolving into a mesmerizing gradient of soft pinks and blues. Amidst the crowd, I felt the brush of bare shoulders and heard the gentle rustle of race bibs, creating a symphony of movement and anticipation. A gunshot cracked through the silence, initiating the start of the race. In perfect synchrony, my heart beat against the walls of my chest, an unwavering drum signaling the start of a thrilling journey ahead.

Inhaling and exhaling deeply, I centered my thoughts and reflected on the countless hours of training that had brought me to this very moment. I silenced the doubts and trusted in my preparation. The time for thinking had passed. Now, it was all about doing what I knew best: running.

There were no amount of breathing techniques that could push the self-doubt from my head for the first 10 miles of the race. I knew how strong and capable my dad and brother believed I was, but I wasn't convinced. I had never done anything like this before and frankly, I was scared. Nevertheless, the miles ticked by one after the other. Twenty miles into the race and to my surprise, I was still running at our goal pace.

The next thing I knew, I was passing the mile 25 banner. My brother ran ahead and finished three minutes faster, but my dad was right by my side. When the finish line was in sight, I reached for his hand and with a last burst of energy, leapt across the chip timer on the asphalt. I had finished my first marathon with an official time of four hours and 10 minutes.

2016
Finishing my first marathon with my dad
Official time: 4:10:38

It's impossible to run a marathon without learning something. That day, I learned that not only shoving two bagels down my throat is not the most ideal pre-marathon breakfast, but also that I could achieve extraordinary accomplishments that had previously surpassed my wildest expectations.

Of course, if someone who never exercises begins training for a marathon, they are going to notice significant changes in their physique and overall fitness. After noticing these effects, I thought that through running—and running alone—I would be able to continue to improve my physique at this same rate.

But here's the thing: progress is not linear; it plateaus when you continue to train at the same intensity. By the end of my first marathon, I had reached that point. In order push past this, I was convinced that I simply needed to run more.

Looking back, I realize that approach was wrong; the secret to elevating my physique lied not in my frequency of running, but my nutrition. Through adequate caloric intake and the addition of strength training exercises, my running performance and physique would have substantially improved.

Sure enough, after several months of undereating and strictly following a regimen of running every day, I was on the brink of burnout and only had minimal physique changes to show for it. I knew that something else needed to change, but I didn't want to admit my approach was wrong. In order to continue running and burning calories, I left behind marching band and joined the cross-country team in my junior year of high school.

The heart of the problem lied in the fact that I have never had a great relationship with food. There have been times when I ate so little that I felt lightheaded and times when I ate so much that I almost threw up. There was simply no middle ground, which left no room for moderation in my eating habits.

It didn't help that around this time, I began modeling. Even though the glitz and glamour of the spotlight was exciting, this pursuit turned out to be more damaging than encouraging. I was already running five miles every day, trying to burn off every calorie I ate, but now I was in an environment where raw vegetables and a bottle of water were considered a meal.

At fashion photoshoots and runway shows, I was surrounded by waif-like women with skinny legs and bony shoulders. I admired their flat stomachs and long, skinny legs. But this flawlessness came at an unhealthy price. No

FINDING FITNESS FREEDOM

eating or drinking for six hours before a show. No cakes or cookies for three weeks leading up to a photoshoot. Makeup must be always perfect. Four-inch heels at a minimum.

My naive mind had crowned these women the epitome of health. You may call this false idolizing, but I saw what I had been trained to see: the modern-day beauty standard. I believed that if I didn't rise to this unnatural benchmark, I simply wasn't good enough to be a model. My self-worth was riding on achieving this standard, and now my modeling career was on the line, too.

2016
Orange County Fashion Week

I set my eyes on the goal and became relentless. I mimicked the model's actions, with the firm belief that if I did exactly what they did I would have the exact same body as them. I decided to take absolute control of my diet, but was overwhelmed by the amount of advice, diets, and strategies out there. It was clear that I would never be able to run off all the calories I was eating, so out of an abundance of caution, I reverted to a simplistic approach: to eat as little as possible.

My mindset was extreme because I thought that was necessary in order to achieve a body like the models I worked with. I wouldn't even take a nibble of something that was conventionally labeled "unhealthy." That meant not even a whiff of cookies, cake, or ice cream. I was convinced that if I had even the smallest amount, it would turn straight into fat.

Over time, my strictness only increased. I added more and more foods to the list of items that I felt were too unhealthy or too calorie dense. Foods that have many nutritional benefits, including potatoes, rice, egg yolks, and cheese all made the list.

I diligently tallied my caloric intake, adding up each meal in my head, and used that as a gauge on how "well" I was doing for the day. I would praise myself for having a breakfast under 200 calories and chide myself for overeating by 100 calories for lunch. To provide an estimate, I was eating between 1,200 and 1,500 calories each day, when I should have been supporting my very active lifestyle with at least 2,000.

During that time, I used calorie counting with a mindset of deprivation, aiming to eat as little as possible, ultimately damaging my self-worth and health in the process. Now, I realize that calorie counting can serve as a beneficial tool for achieving fitness goals. Instead of using calorie counting to deprive myself of food, I use tracking to ensure that I consume enough food to support my strength goals.

Eating so little, I remember feeling lethargic during my long classes in school and physically drained at cross country practice. I struggled to find meals at a restaurant that fit my diet—I mean, how could they? I could barely find foods at a grocery store that were within my dietary restrictions. Because of this, I found myself turning down invites from friends to go to restaurants or parties.

Several months of this behavior and I knew what I was doing was not sustainable for the rest of my life. I needed to change, or my mental and physical health would continue to deteriorate. I decided to eat more, which was a step in the right direction. But no matter how hard I tried, I couldn't change the rigid mindset I had formed on which foods were deemed "safe" for me to consume.

I knew there was something unusual about my eating habits, but it didn't seem accurate to label myself as having an eating disorder. I was sure that my disorder wasn't one of the common ones, like anorexia or bulimia; I didn't throw up my food or starve myself to the bone. However, a couple of google searches led me to discover a much more fitting title to my habits.

When I stumbled upon a condition called "orthorexia nervosa," characterized by having an obsession with healthy eating and restrictive eating behaviors, I felt immense relief. The revelation that this eating disorder existed helped me make sense of everything. Since I had never met another person with the same eating behaviors, I felt alone in my struggle, labeling myself as strange or weird. Learning that other people were going through the same thing brought a strange sense of reassurance.

After high school, I continued my studies at the local community college. Needing motivation to keep running, I joined their cross-country team. Quickly, my schedule was filling up with classes, studying, track meets, and friends. Modeling in fashion shows and doing photoshoots for magazines took the backburner.

Training as an athlete in college, I began to understand the important role nutrition played in athletic performance. I continued to eat from my same pre-approved food list, with the belief that if I ate only "healthy" foods, I could eat as many of them as I wanted and never gain weight. As you will come to realize, this was very untrue.

A couple months of significant overeating, and I began to notice my body getting thicker and more pudgy, particularly on my stomach and legs. Seeing these adverse changes in my body was unexpected and frustrating. I thought my strict diet and excessive running regimen were fool proof, but I was wrong, yet again. "Be honest," I told myself. "You can do better."

Not having enough discipline, I had decided, was what was holding me back from achieving the body of my dreams and the freedom I craved with food.

So, I decided to run even more than I already was. I didn't expect it to be easy; I knew the path to fitness freedom would be grueling and extremely demanding. But if I became unwaveringly disciplined and disregarded how I felt, it would all be worth it in the end, right?

It was the summer of my second year of college, and I had just become introduced to a new group of runners. These were not just any runners; they were ultramarathon runners. It was a group infused with adrenaline and energy, chatting endlessly and singing as they ran from mountaintop to mountaintop. Miles run with them always flew by quicker than I could believe. I met up with them every week after class, and we would traverse through rock-riddled single-track trails, oftentimes in the pitch dark.

Those runners, who called themselves the Wednesday Night Run Club, taught me to embrace "the suck." They taught me that whatever tough thing you were going through, you should be grateful; it could always be a whole hell of a lot worse.

Over the miles, I would overhear their passionate conversations. Sarah had a 50K trail race (31 miles) planned for the summer. Amanda was training for a 50-miler around Catalina Island. Jesse just signed up for his first 100-miler. The mere thought of covering such incredible mileage and the willpower required to achieve such feats, left me in a state of disbelief. Everything they told me defied the limits of what I believed was possible.

It was undeniable that these people were pure crazy. The thing is, I couldn't help but want to be just as crazy.

Running with them week after week, it dawned on me that I wasn't so different from them. They were human. I was human. Why should our abilities be any different? I was easily knocking out 15-mile runs with some of the fastest runners in our group and effortlessly logging 40-50 miles in one week.

2016
My first ultramarathon, The Valencia 50K

We explored the great outdoors on foot, running up and down mountains, traversing single-track trails, soaring down hillsides. Sometimes we were together, sometimes we were alone.

I fell in love with the exhilarating feeling of summiting a mountain and watching the panoramic view unfold before me as I crested the peak. It was during moments like these that I thought back to the hikers from the cover of my science textbook in elementary school. Now, it was *me* standing on the summit—proud, triumphant, alive.

2019
Mt. Baldy Summit, 10,064 feet

One night, I came home after an exhilarating nighttime run, high on endorphins. In the heat of the moment, I went online and opened the site for the Kodiak 50-mile race. I contemplated my decision for a whole five minutes before I impulsively punched the "confirm" button and then sat back in wonder, seriously questioning my sanity.

The Kodiak Ultramarathon was a 50-mile trail race around Big Bear Lake. Already sitting at 7,000 feet above sea level, the race would require 10,000 feet of vertical climbing. I knew what I had signed up to do was insane, but I knew I could do what anyone else could and there were people out there that had run double that distance.

The race started at 4:00 a.m., but I was awake an hour before, filling up water bottles and organizing my backpack with the essentials: salt pills, energy gels, Chapstick, nuts, and Vaseline. The start line was filled with nerves and excitement. Around me, people were hastily making final touches to their gear. My parents were there with me too and helped me pin my bib to my shorts. The ground beneath me was dry silt and I could already feel it tickling my lungs with every deep, calming breath. This was going to be a wild ride.

2019
4:00 a.m. at the start line of the Kodiak 50-Miler

Tiny, white lights bobbed in the distance. I focused on the feet shuffling in front of me, visible only through a yellow tunnel of light emanating from my headlamp. Since everyone had started the race at the same time, the first few miles were full of dodging, weaving, and tripping. The two-foot-wide trail was overcrowded with dirt-churning feet, but I was too high on adrenaline for anything to bother me.

Two hours had flown by in what felt like minutes. Pausing momentarily to look up from the arduous task of concentrating on each footstep, I was greeted with one of the most beautiful sunrises I had ever seen. I watched the light dance over the crest of the mountains and flood the valley below it. The vibrant pinks and purples of the morning sky seemed electric, alive.

Typical marathons have water stations—fold-out plastic tables with hundreds of mini paper cups. Ultramarathons have something called "aid stations," which are water stations on steroids. Aid stations have anything a runner could possibly crave, from baked potatoes rolled in salt to hard candies and peanut M&M's. Luckily, these little pockets of heaven were every six to 10 miles throughout the race.

At the second aid station, I had 20 miles behind me. My parents were massaging my legs, I was chomping down on a peanut-butter and jelly sandwich, and my friend was pointing to a map on his phone, explaining the course that lay ahead of me. I was about to embark on the toughest part of the race: the 3,500-foot climb to the top of Sugarloaf Mountain. I had previously run the mountains around this summit, but didn't expect the rockslides, knotted tree roots, and uneven terrain that awaited me on Sugarloaf. The temperature was also gradually creeping to 80°F.

I wasn't going to let anything scare me. I simply ignored the negative thoughts that wanted to take over my mind and ran my finger along the zip-lock bag in my hand, saving the remaining portions of the sandwich I was nibbling. To my back, I heard my mom call out, "Make that mountain your bitch!" And so, I did.

After summiting the top of Sugarloaf, I was frolicking down the mountain when about half-way down, I ran into some friends from the start line. They were still on the ascent, the towering mountain looming over them. At the start of the race, I had assumed that these two buff dudes were much stronger and better trained than me. Seeing them so far behind was shocking, but also thrilling. I waved to them and continued down the mountain, relishing in the pride of my own abilities.

It turns out that if you don't make it to an aid station in time, you are automatically taken out of the race. I found out later that my friends didn't make it back down the mountain in time and their race ended after reaching the aid station at the bottom of Sugarloaf Mountain.

While the rest of the world was putting on their pajamas and winding down for the day, I was quickly approaching mile 40. I had spent the last 10 hours in the hot, winding trails, being abused by dry shrubbery and assaulted by rocks jutting out of nowhere. I even experienced a hallucination: a neon blue lizard crawling across the trail in front of my feet. It stopped just long enough for me to notice its blue, fluorescent speckled skin. The sun's reflection sparkled off it in kaleidoscopic diamonds as it wiggled through the dirt and off the path. I shook my head, trying to convince myself that I wasn't going crazy, and kept moving.

I was ecstatic to see that my grandmother, along with the rest of my support team, was waiting for me at the mile-43 aid station. She was eager to embrace me in a tight hug, despite my warning about the sweat and smells that were emanating from my body.

2019
My support crew for the Kodiak 50-Miler

The last seven miles were absolute torture, to say the very least. The soles of my feet burned, radiating heat and pain throughout my legs. Everything was chafing to the point of bleeding. My mouth was making sounds that it had never made before; inhuman, guttural moans. I weakly attempted to hold them in but was in too much pain to care what I sounded like. I was in too much pain to care about anything, really.

Nearly three miles away, I thought I could hear the celebratory sounds of the finish line—the sweet sound of ringing cowbells and cheering crowds. I whipped my head to the left and right, arching my neck to see around the turns and twists of the trail in front of me. Yet still, I was greeted by the all too familiar view of towering pine trees and boulders. My ears were hearing what they wanted to hear. There was nothing left to do but keep going.

With one final push, I found myself on the last stretch before the finish line. I saw other runners on the trail in front of me, vomiting, limping, and some nearly collapsing on the ground. In comparison, I didn't feel that bad. I remembered the Wednesday Night Run Club, thinking to myself, *it could always be a whole hell of a lot worse*. Putting on a show of strength and smiling as wide as I could, I leapt over the finish line.

2019
The finish line of the Kodiak 50-Miler

My parents and friends engulfed me in hugs, their tear-streaked faces conveying an overwhelming mix of pride, relief, and shared accomplishment. The air was charged with an electric energy, crackling with unspoken words and uncontainable emotions. It was as if time stood still, the culmination of months of training and stubborn determination converging into a single, glorious moment. The weight of my achievement finally settled upon my shoulders, a triumphant melody that etched itself into the tapestry of my memory, forever marking the day that I ran fifty miles in fourteen hours and thirty minutes.

The race director emerged from the crowd and hung a sparkling medal around my neck. She asked how old I was and when I told her I was 19, she said that I was the youngest person to finish her race.

After the initial excitement wore off, I realized that I had dirt everywhere. My dad, bless his heart, went to work immediately. He peeled my sweat-drenched socks off and revealed my feet, caked black with grime. The only thing that would be able to clean my feet was a power wash and two buckets of soap, but his persistent wipes got a surprising amount of gunk off.

Finishing the Kodiak 50-Miler had attracted the attention of local fitness brands, leading to sponsorships with Two Times You and Fabletics. Eager to have a passionate ultramarathon runner join their team, I started a new job at my favorite running watch company, COROS Wearables.

At school, when teachers and classmates would ask me what I did over summer break, I'd proudly say, "I ran an ultramarathon." Usually, their response was, "An ultramarathon? What's that?" In which I would reply, "Any race longer than a marathon."

The conversation usually unfolded to reveal that I had run 50 miles in one day. The astonishment reflected in their widened eyes and gaping mouths, accompanied by my repeated emphasis of, "Yes, five zero," left no doubt that I was a complete and total badass. But here's the thing: no one wants to admit their weaknesses, especially not complete and total badasses.

My weakness, I had decided, was too embarrassing and unbelievable to confess. More than that, I was terrified to admit it to myself and risk facing the undeniable truth. After running the longest and most grueling race of my life, I felt indestructible. But as the thrill of my accomplishment wound down and I went back to life as an average college student, it was back to reality, where my insecurity made itself unrelentingly present.

I couldn't do a single push-up.

I just ran 50 miles through the rugged mountains of Big Bear, climbing 4,000 feet up mountains and traversing across rockslides, but I couldn't do a push-up? Not even one? There was something seriously wrong with this picture.

It was clear that I was missing a key piece of the puzzle, and it wasn't easy to admit. I was talking to friends and family like I had fitness all figured out. But there I was, not able to do something that most of the population could do without any training at all. I felt like an imposter, a fraud.

The New Year came around and I had set even loftier goals for 2020. Once again, I found myself on the Kodiak Ultramarathons website, but this time, I chose the 100-mile distance. There were several races I had planned to help me train, but I had my eyes on the prize. I knew 100 miles was a lofty goal, but then again, so was 50 miles just last year. What would be 50 more?

It was mid-March when I got the news that my classmates and I wouldn't be returning after spring break. At first, I was excited for the extra time off from college. Little did I know, the COVID-19 lockdown, which would last for more than a year, had begun.

The weeks went by, and school still had not resumed. Of course, most everyone was relentlessly optimistic that life would soon return to normal. It wasn't until a month or two later, when emails from race directors began flooding my inbox, that I started to panic. Every race had been canceled.

My whole world was suddenly put on pause. I wasn't the only one who was devastated by this sudden change of events, but because I relied so heavily on running races as my main source of exercise, I worried that I was going to lose my fitness progress and hard-earned physique. These races were my motivation to continue training and without them, I was scared I would let it all go.

FINDING FITNESS FREEDOM

My college classes had all been moved online, but I still found myself with a lot of free time. Instead of going on social media or succumbing to the comfort of my couch and a mindless reality TV show, I decided to take my life in my own hands. I wanted to use this new-found time to improve myself, starting in the area that I was weakest.

My goal was simple: to do a single push-up from my toes with perfect form. I knew it would require a dramatic change in my workout routine, but I faced the challenge head-on.

2020
Attempting a push-up, and not able to lift myself off the ground

There was only one problem. I didn't have access to a gym or any equipment. Suddenly, I remembered an Amazon purchase I had made years back with the intention of adding resistance to my core workouts. Running upstairs to my closet, I excavated my one and only pair of dumbbells. Underneath a thick layer of dust, you could make out the numbers on each side: eight pounds. That would work.

My workouts were made up of whatever I could do with that single pair of dumbbells. Bicep curls, bench press from the floor, and standing overhead press. For other exercises, I relied on my own body weight, like elevated push-ups, squats, and lunges. It was clear that I had no idea what I was doing, but I didn't really care. I knew I had a lot to learn, and I had all the time in the world to practice.

I was used to fast-paced cardiovascular exercise, like sprinting up hills or running 10 miles at a time. Strength training was not about going fast, in fact, it was quite the opposite. I moved through the exercises methodically, focusing on feeling each muscle contract. I would spend several minutes in between sets simply resting, doing nothing. I was uncomfortable with such long periods of doing "nothing" during my workouts. But I knew my muscles needed proper rest, so they could give their all in the next set.

Experimenting with weights didn't stop my running routine, but it did change it. I figured that if I balanced weightlifting with cardio, I would be able to maintain the same physique I had currently, while still exploring a new form of exercise.

Since I was home alone, I surrounded myself with online inspiration. My social media pages narrowed to encompass only educators and strong female influencers. I wanted to scroll through my feed on Instagram and learn something about how to get stronger instead of seeing frail women model in dresses smaller than a sandal. I thoroughly immersed myself in the world of weightlifting, spending hours on fitness forums and reading educational books.

After a month of learning about this "new" way to exercise and putting it to practice, I began to notice surprising changes in my body composition. Muscles were peeking out of places they had never before and clothes were fitting tighter, especially in my chest and arms. My abs were visible, making small ripples down my stomach. These were exciting changes in my body; changes I had never experienced through any other type of exercise.

Throughout most of my life, I held steadfast to the belief that having a body like the one I dreamed of was only achievable through a rigorous workout routine and strict, restrictive dieting. I had always thought I wasn't pushing myself hard enough or being strict enough with my diet. Now that I can recognize the flawed and extremely damaging nature of that mindset, I am able to find the silver lining and realize that having such strictness played an integral role in shaping the unwavering discipline that I have today.

When I commit to something, it's like there's a fire lit within me; I cannot stop until I complete what I set out to do. I sign up for a 50-mile race, I run it; I start writing a book, I finish it. I push through any challenge because the rewards of completion far outweigh the costs of working hard.

This mindset became deeply rooted in me through years of cultivating self-discipline both mentally and physically. Having believed for a lifetime that there existed only a singular path to attain the physique I desired, the notion of reducing my exercise duration by incorporating weight training felt contradictory. This was why it was almost impossible for me to believe that what I was doing with my weights in the backyard was working.

I was making progress towards my first push-up, but not enough. I knew that in order to get stronger, I needed to be lifting heavier. But how do you get more equipment in the middle of a global pandemic? Every store, including online markets, were sold out. Apparently, I wasn't the only one with the plan to use my free time working out. My dad, who would peek his head out in the backyard occasionally to see what I was doing, noticed my struggle in finding more equipment and offered to help.

After one trip to the local hardware store, he came home with a pipe and several square blocks of wood. In the garage, he went to drilling and hammering, bits of splintered wood flying around the workspace. When I came over to see what he was working on, I saw that he had drilled holes in the middle of each block of wood and threaded them through the metal pipe. It was a wooden weighted barbell.

I began using that barbell in every workout. It allowed me to adjust the number of wooden blocks to the ends, so I could now choose whatever weight I wanted. The next several months were productive and my strength was gradually improving.

2020
The wooden barbell my dad made during the COVID-19 pandemic

Two months into my push-up training and it was time to put my efforts to the test. I set up my camera against a wall in my backyard and hit record. Whatever happened, I was going to have footage of it. I thought, either I do my first push-up and this moment will go down in history, or I fail, and I'll have a video to look back on for when I can do a push-up. I was so dedicated to my practice that I didn't care if I failed today; I'd try again tomorrow.

I got in a plank position. With my toes digging into the concrete, I let my arms lower me until I was at the bottom of the push-up, and then pushed with all my might. That day, I did not do a push-up. I did seven.

Doing my first push-up was monumental, but seven push-ups was beyond what I ever expected. I had proven to myself, once again, that I could accomplish something that took consistency and work.

Even though I had accomplished so much with my running achievements, this feeling was somehow different and more powerful. I had transformed my upper body—something that had been a weakness for my entire life—into my strength. But I wasn't ready to stop. I already had my mind set on the next goal: a single, unassisted pull-up.

FINDING FITNESS FREEDOM

Before I knew it, it was 2021. By that point, I had made major upgrades to my home gym, including relocating it to the garage. This was much better, because not only was it an enclosed space, but it had mirrors, lights, and speakers. I could play any music I wanted, which made workouts feel like dance parties. However, the best part about this new gym was my brother's makeshift pull-up bar.

Every single day, I dedicated myself to practicing on that bar. Finally, after months of relentless effort, I achieved another significant milestone: one full pull-up.

I found myself addicted to the pursuit of strength, constantly yearning to unlock higher levels of power and capability. Gradually, I began to experience the metaphorical—and literal—feeling of a weight being lifted as I discovered what fitness freedom felt like. I had not only created a new passion for myself, but I had created a new way of living. I was fitter than I had ever been before, but I wasn't working harder, I was working smarter.

My transformation
Left: 2016, 115 pounds
Right: 2023, 145 pounds

I spent my whole life trying to find out how to create a balance between health, enjoyment of food, and being proud of the way my body looked. After I gained muscle mass and witnessed its power to transform my relationship with food and build my physique, I deeply yearned to tell my past self that the damaging mindset I had employed for years was unnecessary. It wasn't because I wasn't disciplined enough; I simply lacked the knowledge necessary to find fitness freedom.

Then I thought about the fact that most women hadn't gone through the emotional and physical journey that I had. In fact, most women were still stuck in the frustrating hamster wheel of crash dieting and cardio-focused workouts; regimens that I fell victim to believing would revolutionize my physique. I suddenly felt as if I was withholding a secret from everyone. I wanted to scream it from the rooftops: *Lifting weights! That's the answer!*

The frustration of not being able to get my message across by literally screaming from the rooftops fueled my decision to take my education to the next level. While balancing a full-time undergraduate course load, I became a certified personal trainer through the National Academy of Sports Medicine (NASM). Soon after, I finished my last semester at community college and transferred to a university.

Everything was lining up perfectly. Within one month of receiving my acceptance letter from California State University, Long Beach, I signed the lease on my first apartment. In the middle of the moving process, I applied to be a personal trainer at a local gym, Iconix Fitness. One week and several persistent emails later, I was hired.

Becoming a personal trainer felt like a natural progression that aligned perfectly with my major. Biology encompasses the fundamental building blocks of life, including the composition of our bodies, from our skin to our bones, tendons, and muscles. It's within these structures that the magic of human movement and physical transformation takes place. Leveraging my understanding of biology and my recent fitness transformation, I was confident I could help others reach any goal they desired.

Working at Iconix was exactly what I needed to start my training career. I embraced the opportunity to learn from the knowledgeable team of experts, constantly seeking their guidance and always asking questions. Monthly meetings and team bonding activities helped establish that this wasn't just a job, it was a community, and I was immediately welcomed with open arms.

Before long, a year had passed, and I had built a long list of dedicated clients with whom I made strong connections. My coworkers and clients even gave me presents on my birthdays and asked about my family. In fact, some client relationships were so strong that we remain good friends to this day.

2023
Doing what I love as a trainer at Iconix Fitness

Even though I was changing lives, I still couldn't help but feel like I wasn't doing enough. My inbox was filling up with messages from friends, family members, and even people I didn't know on social media, all begging for me to help them achieve their fitness goals. With my strict obligation to the club, potential clients had to live in the same city as me. On top of that, they had to be willing to pay the membership fee and the training fee. I felt out of reach to many people who needed help.

After many months of research, I finally figured out how to take my training services online without sacrificing the quality of their experience. In December of 2022, I launched the Bright Fitness app.

It was simple. Clients simply had to download my app, answer a couple of personalized questions, and they instantly had access to their customized workout program. No longer were clients restricted to training with me at my own private gym. They could workout anytime and anywhere, with any equipment they had available. This was a monumental shift in my career, as I was no longer restricted to being an in-person coach for a small fitness club. I was accessible to anyone in the world.

In the remarkably short span of just a couple of months since launching my online platform, I witnessed the transformative power it held. It became a catalyst for forging meaningful connections and instigating positive shifts in people's habits. Interestingly, I discovered that many of my clients shared common backgrounds and relatable experiences when it came to exercise and fitness. Through my guidance, they began to unravel their untapped potential by embracing the art of weightlifting.

It was during a trip to my local bookstore that a moment of clarity struck me like a lightning bolt. It became evident that the impact I could make extended far beyond the boundaries of my online platform and it was time to embark on an exciting new chapter of my mission.

During that trip to the store, I noticed a disturbing trend in the "women's health and fitness" section. The titles on the books were unquestionably directed towards women. *Pilates: A Workout for Women, The Yoga Solution, Fitness for Females over Fifty*. I only had one question: what was so different about women's workouts as compared to men's workouts?

Cracking open their spines, I was offended by the advice that was spewing from the pages. Between the covers, there was a slurry of incorrect form advice and a compilation of fad diets all aimed at helping women lose that "pesky belly fat." There was weightlifting advice, but each exercise was aimed at a particular fatty spot on the body, claiming that they could "spot reduce fat" with pink five-pound dumbbells and jump ropes.

Appalled, I fled the store, confused and slightly angry. Those books were being sold at a bookstore and that was the best advice they could offer? Didn't anyone write a book that encouraged women to gain muscle through lifting heavy weights? Dare I say, weights as heavy as the men's?

As I drove home that evening, I got more and more upset. I couldn't stop thinking about everything I wanted to say to the authors of those books. Those authors were perpetuating the old narrative that women should be small, dainty, and petite, distracting 50% of the population with foofoo tips and tricks.

Two years ago, I would have believed everything and anything I read in those books, written by exercise specialists and personal trainers. If I hadn't gone through my own transformative fitness journey, I would probably still be sitting in that store, reading paragraph after paragraph of those false and misleading books.

Later that evening, I reflected on my own complicated history with exercise and my many exhausting attempts at finding fitness freedom. Running numerous ultramarathons with the hope that I would be able to eat anything I wanted after my race. Eating very little and being afraid that any "unhealthy" food would turn straight to fat. Believing I wasn't as beautiful as other women simply because I didn't have a physique like them.

The epiphany I experienced after my first month of lifting weights was not meant to be only for me. I had freedom with food and exercise, allowing me to relax at dinner parties and cherish time with friends more. That freedom is something everyone deserves to have.

Suddenly, it occurred to me: I should write my own book. Instead of trying to lure susceptible women into believing fad diets and quick fixes, this book would reveal the truth about how to become your best self, physically and emotionally. It would be real, raw, and unfiltered, but most importantly, it would illuminate the path to finding fitness freedom.

This book is a comprehensive roadmap that will forever change the way you perceive exercise, food, and your overall well-being. It's a journey dedicated to shattering long-standing myths and misconceptions surrounding women and weightlifting, ultimately paving the way for a new era of purpose and empowerment.

You know my story; you know what I've been through. If there's anything I want you to take away from all of this, it's that you are capable of so much more than you realize. We are all human beings and if I can do something, there is no doubt that you can do it too.

This is not merely a book; it's a catalyst for your own personal discovery. With every turn of the page, you are taking an active role in your own personal growth and development. Embrace the freedom and responsibility that come with it. Your journey is a testament to your unique potential, and the possibilities that lie ahead are boundless.

FINDING FITNESS FREEDOM

ple
A BRIEF HISTORY OF WOMEN AND EXERCISE

Throughout history, men were expected to maintain physical fitness for hunting, warfare, and other demanding tasks. Meanwhile, women were confined to domestic roles, like caring for children and maintaining the household. Because of this separation, society promoted the image of women as delicate and frail, emphasizing qualities of daintiness and femininity. It wasn't until recent decades that women began to receive encouragement to engage in physical exercise.

The 1920s, often referred to as the "Roaring Twenties" or the "Jazz Age," witnessed a wave of societal changes, including the women's suffrage. In terms of fitness, this period marked a departure from the traditional Victorian ideals that emphasized modesty, restraint, and the relegation of women to domestic roles.

Rather than emphasizing strength, women's physical activities during this period primarily focused on achieving a more slender figure. Dance became an increasingly popular form of exercise, with the emergence of energetic dance styles like the Charleston and the Black Bottom. These dances not only provided a means of exercise, but also allowed women to express themselves and embrace a sense of liberation.

In addition to dancing, swimming, tennis, golf, and horseback riding began gaining popularity among women. Typically done in heels and dresses, these activities were seen as both recreational and beneficial for physical well-being. In order to promote and organize these activities, women's sports clubs and athletic associations were established.

Publications and magazines of the time, such as Women's Home Companion and Good Housekeeping, started featuring articles on health, exercise, and maintaining a youthful appearance. They provided advice on diet, beauty, and exercise routines specifically targeted towards women.

Even though the focus of fitness for women in the 1920s was still associated with maintaining an attractive appearance rather than focusing on overall health and strength, it laid the foundation for future generations to challenge traditional gender roles and embrace more inclusive and diverse perspectives on fitness and physical well-being.

Fitness for women in the 1940s was greatly influenced by the events and social changes brought about by World War II. With many men enlisted in the military, women assumed new roles in society, including the workforce and various military support roles. This shift in responsibilities also influenced the perception and practice of fitness during that era.

Many women participated in physical fitness programs offered by organizations like the Young Women's Christian Association (YWCA) and the American Red Cross. These programs aimed to improve women's strength, endurance, and overall fitness levels through exercise classes and recreational activities like swimming, hiking, and cycling. Women's sports clubs gained popularity, providing opportunities for participation in team sports such as basketball, softball, and volleyball.

Also popular during this time were calisthenics and group exercise classes that emphasized repetitive, bodyweight exercises. Women would gather in community centers, gyms, or outdoor spaces to do exercises that focused on flexibility, strength, and cardiovascular fitness—no longer wearing heels and dresses, but bloomers or one-pieces instead. Common exercises were jumping jacks, squats, and lunges.

Following the end of World War II, the 1950s marked a return to a more traditional gender role division, with women primarily being encouraged to focus on their roles as wives and mothers. As a result, fitness for women during this period revolved around maintaining an attractive and feminine appearance rather than pursuing athletic pursuits or intense physical training. In pursuit of the idealized image of the "perfect housewife," women were encouraged to do activities that would help them achieve and maintain an hourglass figure, with a narrow waist and rounded hips.

However, calisthenics and dance exercises remained popular fitness options for women. Exercise routines and dance classes, such as ballet, were promoted as a means to stay in shape and improve posture. These activities were deemed appropriate for women and aligned with the ideal feminine image of grace and elegance.

Home exercise programs and equipment began gaining popularity, encouraging women to use equipment such as hula hoops, vibrating belt machines, and simple exercise tools like resistance bands to tone their bodies. Magazines and advertisements often featured products and routines that promised to help women achieve the desired physique without significant effort. One of these products was called the Vibro-Slim, a machine that claimed to "melt fat off bodies" simply by vibrating and jiggling a woman's fatty areas.

1965
Members of the Bluebell Dancing troop show
how to use the Vibro-Slim in a Paris beauty parlor

Nutrition was also promoted as an essential aspect of fitness. Women were advised to watch their caloric intake, limit indulgences, and choose low-fat foods to maintain their desired figure.

It's important to note that while fitness in the 1950s focused on physical appearance, some women continued to participate in sports and physical activities outside of traditional expectations. However, their visibility and recognition were limited compared to men's sports during that era.

For those who wanted to continue exercising, Jack LaLanne made a lasting impact through his influential television show, "The Jack LaLanne Show." He recognized that women had unique fitness needs and aspirations, and he tailored his workouts and advice specifically for them. His inclusive approach resonated with women from all walks of life, empowering them to take control of their bodies and embrace a healthier lifestyle.

During a time when women's exercise routines were limited to gentle calisthenics or stretching, LaLanne introduced dynamic and energetic workouts that showcased women's potential for strength and endurance. While these workouts were considered easier in comparison to men's workouts, they were instrumental in shifting the narrative around women's fitness. LaLanne's efforts were remarkable in challenging the status quo and introducing women to a more active and empowered approach to fitness.

In the 1960s, more women took to exercise, but sports participation for women was still limited, discouraged, and considered unfeminine. However, some women began to challenge these stereotypes. Notable examples include Althea Gibson, who broke racial barriers as the first African American woman to compete in professional tennis, and Wilma Rudolph, an Olympic sprinter who became an inspiration for female athletes.

In the 1970s and 1980s, the feminist movement was gaining momentum, challenging traditional gender roles and advocating for women's empowerment. This cultural shift had a significant impact, as women began advocating for their right to participate in sports and fitness pursuits.

During this time, aerobic exercise was quickly gaining popularity, thanks in part to influential figures like Jane Fonda. Her aerobics videos, such as "Jane Fonda's Original Workout," encouraged women to engage in high-energy, dance-inspired exercises that aimed to improve cardiovascular fitness and overall health. The release of Olivia Newton John's hit single, "Let's Get Physical" also helped to draw attention to exercise.

The aerobic craze sparked a fitness movement, with many women going to exercise classes, joining fitness clubs, and incorporating more physical activity into their daily routines. Flaunting their belted leotards, headbands, and leg warmers, women fully embracing their femininity and newfound strength.

1982
Jane Fonda's Original Workout DVD

In the background of this aerobics movement, men's professional bodybuilding was becoming popular. Icons like Arnold Schwarzenegger and Bill Pearl were just beginning their competition career. Notable contests in these early years of bodybuilding included the Mr. America competition and the Mr. Universe competition.

Prior to the 1980s, weightlifting was predominantly seen as a male-dominated activity, but bodybuilding competitions encouraged everyone to lift. The inclusion of women's weightlifting as an Olympic sport further highlighted the growing recognition and acceptance of women's strength and athletic abilities.

Among the first ladies to break the mold were Rachel McLish, the Ms. Olympia bodybuilder in 1980, as well as Bev Francis, Cory Everson, and Carla Dunlap. These women were among the first to establish a "new" physique that quickly became desired. More women took to bodybuilding and new divisions in pro bodybuilding competitions emerged, like the International Fitness and Bodybuilding Federation (IFBB) and National Physique Committee (NPC). Despite this inclusion, these divisions gained momentum slowly, for only a select few women wholeheartedly embraced the world of bodybuilding.

2010
Sonia Gonzalez, Ms. Bikini Olympia
Photographed by Dan Ray

In order to provide a broader range of physical activity options for women, the 1990s and 2000s fitness landscape experienced a shift towards cardio-based activities. This period witnessed the surge of dancing, running, and cycling, gaining significant popularity among women seeking fun and effective ways to stay fit.

One notable fitness trend that emerged was the creation of Zumba. Developed in the mid-1990s by Colombian dancer and choreographer Alberto Perez, Zumba combined Latin dance rhythms with aerobic exercises. This dynamic and energetic workout quickly became famous worldwide, appealing to people of all ages and fitness levels. Zumba classes offered an enjoyable and social way to burn calories, improve cardiovascular fitness, and showcase dance moves inspired by Latin music.

The combined influence of Zumba and the official recognition of women's weightlifting in the Olympics contributed to a more diverse and inclusive fitness culture during the 1990s and 2000s. Women had an expanding range of options to choose from when it came to exercise, whether they preferred high-energy dance workouts or strength-based activities like weightlifting. These trends encouraged women to explore a wide range of fitness modalities, challenge traditional gender stereotypes, and embrace their physical capabilities in new and exciting ways.

Despite the ever-changing trends in workout preferences, one thing had become clear: women were capable of being strong and muscular. In fact, women's bodybuilding had gained enough momentum for the NPC and IFBB pro bodybuilding competitions to develop a new "Bikini" division. In 2010, Sonia Gonzalez won the first ever Ms. Bikini Olympia, one of the most prestigious bodybuilding events in the world.

It was clear that bodybuilding required intense dedication and hard work. Many women were hesitant to invest the countless hours and grueling workouts necessary to achieve a physique associated with traditional bodybuilding ideals. Instead, there emerged a preference for a different kind of physique, one that was deemed more attainable and desirable. This was perpetuated by the media landscape of the 2000s, which prominently featured supermodels like Jodie Kidd, Kaia Gerber, and Kendall Kardashian.

These supermodels epitomized a notion that women should maintain a fragile and petite image, prioritizing a slender and lightweight frame. They were celebrated for their miniscule 23-inch waists and body weights as low as 100 pounds. This portrayal promoted the belief that women should strive for a delicate aesthetic.

It is within this context that women faced conflicting messages and societal pressures. On one hand, the rise of women's bodybuilding showcased the potential for strength and muscularity. On the other hand, the prevailing media representations of supermodels emphasized a different, more fragile ideal.

2003
Jodie Kidd at a Roland Klein fashion show

These contrasting influences posed a challenge for women seeking to define their own fitness journeys. The path to achieving a desirable physique seemed to be paved with conflicting expectations and misconceptions. Women were left questioning which path to pursue, grappling with a desire for strength, empowerment, and self-acceptance, while simultaneously contending with societal pressures to conform to narrowly defined beauty standards.

Amidst this complex landscape, a powerful realization emerged: lifting weights does not equate to bulking up. Rather, it has the power to transform the body and mind into their leanest and fiercest forms. This powerful understanding allows us to redefine the landscape of strength and dispel the myths and stereotypes that once limited women's potential.

Gone are the days of extreme diets and excessive workouts. Through embracing weightlifting, we unlock a trove of physical and mental benefits, from developing lean muscle mass and enhancing bone density to revving up metabolism and bolstering overall strength. With this discovery, comes the understanding that weightlifting can be a catalyst for self-discovery and self-acceptance.

In the big picture, women lifting weights is not simply about individual progress, but a paradigm shift in the perception of femininity, capabilities, and personal empowerment. With that said, it is our collective responsibility to nurture and amplify the voices of women in the weightlifting community, ensuring that their accomplishments and contributions are recognized and celebrated. In doing so, we foster an environment where women of all backgrounds can thrive, inspire, and pave the way for future generations.

It's time we redefine the narrative surrounding strength training and demonstrate that lifting weights is not solely the domain of men. We have work to do.

03
EVERYONE SHOULD LIFT WEIGHTS

FINDING FITNESS FREEDOM

In a world where fitness trends come and go, the timeless sport of weightlifting stands tall as a pillar of strength and vitality. While this book focuses on introducing women to lifting weights, this transformative practice transcends age and gender, offering benefits that are universally accessible for everyone.

I like to think of weightlifting as an art form that taps into the depths of our physical potential. By engaging in strength training, we push ourselves to overcome obstacles, both internal and external, and discover reservoirs of strength within us. Through this process, we learn valuable lessons about perseverance and discipline.

While the external benefits of weightlifting are evident in the development of muscular strength and improved body composition, the internal advantages are equally significant. Regular strength training has been proven to boost metabolism, increase bone density, and enhance cardiovascular health. Moreover, weightlifting promotes functional fitness, enabling us to perform everyday tasks with greater ease and with a reduced risk of injury.

It wasn't until a couple of months of consistent strength training that I started to notice significant changes in my physique. I weighed more but looked better. It seemed contradictory, but I couldn't argue with what I was feeling. Fat was no longer in places where there used to be fat, muscles were giving my body shape, and I was doing exercises I never thought I'd be able to do. The feeling of accomplishment that followed each achievement had made my confidence higher than ever before.

Many years of self-reflection has allowed me to come to the realization that the ideal feminine physique is not one that is confined to a low number on the scale. It's one that resonates with your own confidence, radiates strength, and embodies health. It's one that relishes in the thrill of conquering strenuous hikes, dancing for hours at parties, and confidently wearing bikinis at the beach. You'll find that when you possess this level of self-assurance, your attention naturally shifts away from materialistic possessions, for there's no amount of shoes or jewelry that can buy true confidence.

To reach this state, you must incorporate heavy weights into your routine along with proper nutrition. The act of lifting weights will not only shape and sculpt your physique, but it also will empower you to push beyond your perceived limits. With each session, you build not only physical strength, but also something called "mental toughness," which enables you to tackle any challenge that comes your way. The discipline and focus required to excel in weightlifting will transfer to all other areas of your life, allowing you to face challenges and persevere in the pursuit of your goals.

In the pages ahead, I will explore the many physiological, psychological, and emotional dimensions of this transformative practice. Whether you seek to build strength, enhance your physique, boost your confidence, or simply embrace a healthier lifestyle, weightlifting offers a multifaceted approach to personal growth and self-improvement.

BODY RECOMPOSITION

When it comes to fitness, the goal should never be "to be skinnier." The notion of being skinny carries connotations of being small and frail, which is contradictory to being strong and healthy.

Now, I understand where the desire to be skinny stems from. In a world consumed by numbers—be it the scale or the measuring tape—we often find ourselves desperate to conform to societal expectations. This causes many people to resort to extreme measures like restrictive diets and excessive exercising. But what if I told you there's a path less traveled, one that holds far greater rewards?

Along this less-traveled route, you'll discover the remarkable truth that building more muscle and strength naturally leads to a body composition characterized by lower body fat, a faster metabolism, and a beautifully sculpted physique. This is called body recomposition, or "body recomp," the simultaneous process of gaining lean muscle mass and losing body fat.

When you lift heavy weights, your body is met with resistance that stimulates and ignites the growth of muscle fibers. This is initiated as you break down muscle fibers during a lifting session, which causes the calories you consume throughout the day to be directed towards the noble task of rebuilding those fibers. Not only do the muscles rebuild, but they come back stronger and more resilient than before. Ensuring an adequate intake of protein allows the muscles to repair and rebuild themselves at maximum efficiency.

That's the beauty of the art of muscle building—each time you challenge your body, it responds by constructing a sturdier foundation, fostering the growth and development of lean muscle mass. To make the deal even sweeter, muscle mass is incredibly metabolically active, meaning it burns a significant number of calories simply by existing. This means as muscle mass increases, your body is more able to utilize stored fat as an energy source, reducing your total body fat.

Conversely, individuals who neglect weightlifting or fail to challenge their muscles regularly may notice that any excess calories they consume will be stored as fat. On the other hand, those who incorporate weightlifting into their routines while consuming a consistent amount of calories are more likely to witness the transformation of their physique, becoming more muscular and leaner in the process.

In order to achieve successful body recomposition, a well-balanced diet is necessary. Consuming sufficient protein, to support muscle growth and repair, in addition to maintaining a slight caloric deficit is needed in order to lose fat. We will go into more detail about how to feed your body to support your fitness goals in chapter nine.

It's also important to note that body recomposition is a gradual process that requires consistency, dedication, and patience. Progress may vary depending on individual factors such as genetics, current body composition, and training intensity. Regular monitoring of body measurements, such as body fat percentage and muscle mass, can help track progress and make necessary adjustments to training and nutrition plans.

As a beginner, think of body recomposition as your superpower. The absence of a substantial muscle base presents a unique advantage, as the body is primed to respond eagerly to the stimuli of proper exercise and nourishment. By engaging in a targeted training routine that combines resistance exercises and cardiovascular activities, you'll effectively stimulate muscle growth and ignite the fat-shedding process.

By combining strength training exercises, proper nutrition, and a focus on both muscle gain and fat loss, you can achieve a balanced and lean physique while improving your overall health and well-being.

INJURIES

Picture this: you're out on a run, feeling the wind in your hair and the pavement beneath your feet. Suddenly, a sharp pain shoots through your knee, forcing you to halt your stride. It's a frustrating setback known as "runner's knee," a common injury that can derail even the most dedicated fitness enthusiasts. The frustration of experiencing an injury and being forced to take time off to heal sets in—an all-too-familiar setback among runners.

Now, shift your focus to the tennis court—or pickleball court—you eagerly anticipate the satisfying thwack of the ball against your racket. However, as you execute a powerful swing, a persistent ache flares up in your elbow, casting a shadow over your competitive spirit. This lingering ailment, known as "tennis elbow," can significantly impede your performance and dampen the joy you derive from the sport you love.

Injuries due to underdeveloped muscles or improper form can arise in any activity, whether that's baseball, soccer, volleyball, cycling, bowling, or hockey. Luckily, there is a solution that will help you avoid these obstacles and enjoy a more injury-resistant life. Surprisingly, it doesn't have to do with changing your warm-up routine or doing more effective stretches. Rather, it lies in the strength of your muscles and their connective tissues.

Everyone knows that strength training increases strength, but what they may not realize is that it goes far beyond mere muscle building. The human body is a complex web of interconnected components, including tendons and ligaments, which work together to support movement and physical function. These connective tissues provide critical stability to the joints, helping to maintain proper alignment and range of motion. They act as robust connectors between muscles and bones, ensuring efficient force transmission during movement.

When stress is placed on the body through strength training, a synergistic collaboration occurs among the muscles, tendons, and ligaments to generate force. As these tissues work together harmoniously, they stimulate the development of a more robust network of interconnecting tissues. This intricate interplay contributes to a heightened level of strength, stability, and resilience throughout your body, reducing the likelihood of sprains, strains, and other joint-related injuries.

Moreover, strength training contributes to bone health and density. The controlled stress placed on the bones during resistance exercises stimulates the body's natural bone remodeling process. Over time, this leads to increased bone mineral density, making your skeletal structure more resilient and less prone to fractures or osteoporosis. We will go more into the mechanics of this process in the next section.

That means that through regular strength training, you create a protective shield around your body's more vulnerable areas. The strengthened musculature acts as a safeguard, absorbing impact and minimizing stress on joints, tendons, and ligaments. This enhanced support allows you to perform daily activities with greater ease, participate in sports or physical activities more effectively, and reduce the risk of overuse injuries.

Incorporating strength training into your routine is incredibly rewarding, as it allows you to tap into your true potential while steering clear of the frustrating setbacks caused by injuries. By prioritizing safe and effective strength training techniques, you pave the way for a journey that is both fulfilling and injury-free, unlocking the door to your optimal performance.

BONE HEALTH

The human body is remarkable, capable of adapting and responding to a wide range of stimuli. Among its incredible capabilities is the ability of bone tissue to strengthen in response to exercise.

As we age, we experience a natural decline in bone density. In fact, once we approach the age of fifty, the pace at which we lose bone density surpasses our ability to build it. This disparity becomes even more pronounced in women, who can experience a staggering loss of up to 20% of their bone density within a mere span of five to seven years after reaching menopause [20]. This is due to female hormonal changes and a less muscle mass.

It is within this context that we recognize the critical importance of incorporating measures to support and enhance bone health, ensuring the longevity and vitality of our skeletal system. Luckily, there is a lot you can do to keep your bones healthy and strong as you age. In fact, emerging evidence has shown that through weightlifting, we can reverse the process of bone loss [10].

When we weightlift, the application of resistance and tension on our muscles exerts a remarkable force on our skeletal system. This force stimulates the bones to respond by producing more bone tissue, a phenomenon known as bone remodeling. The mechanical stress placed on the bones during weightlifting triggers a cascade of physiological processes that promote bone formation, strengthening the skeletal structure in the process.

In addition to directly influencing bone density, weightlifting offers a range of additional benefits that synergistically contribute to overall bone health. One such benefit is the improvement of balance and coordination, vital factors in preventing falls and subsequent fractures, particularly among older individuals who may face challenges in recovering from such injuries.

Considering the significant impact that regular strength training has on bone health, it's abundantly clear that lifting weights should be a vital component of any comprehensive fitness regimen, particularly for older adults. By prioritizing weightlifting and incorporating it into their routine, you can actively combat age-related bone density decline, safeguarding your skeletal health and promoting a long, fracture-free life.

STRESS MANAGEMENT

In addition to physical strength, weightlifting can play a big part in fortifying our mental health. Think of the iron we lift in the gym as a metaphorical weight that trains our minds to overcome any obstacle and push through adversity.

It's well known that dealing with stress is toxic to multiple systems in the body. In fact, too much stress can lead to medical diagnoses like high blood pressure and a weakened immune system. A plethora of mental illnesses accompany these ailments, such as anxiety and depression. In order to avoid these complications, you must understand the link between stress and exercise.

Physical stress can be experienced by exercising, like lifting heavy weights, running, or playing a sport. Initially, these activities engage the stress response in the body. However, people typically experience lower levels of the harmful stress hormones, like cortisol and epinephrine. On the other hand, exercise increases the amount of norepinephrine, an important neuromodulator that helps the brain deal with stress more efficiently. Thus, through exercise, you can train your brain to become more prepared when it encounters other similar forms of stress.

You can think of it as physical stress mimicking all other types of stress. This is because when you subject your body to any type of stress, the physiological systems involved in the response are forced to communicate much more closely than usual. In this way, exercise is a practice round for the real deal and those who exercise regularly are going to be better equipped to handle stressful or difficult situations.

SLEEP QUALITY

If you have difficulty sleeping at night, you're not alone. Numerous studies have revealed that insomnia affects a significant portion of the population, ranging from 10% to 30%.

Fortunately, there's great news: engaging in moderate exercise can significantly enhance the quality of your sleep. It can reduce the time it takes to fall asleep and minimize the instances of being awake in bed during the night. Additionally, physical activity can reduce daytime sleepiness and the reliance on sleep medications.

In 2003, the National Sleep Foundation conducted a survey targeting adults aged 55 to 84. The results indicated that 52% exercised three or more times per week, while 24% exercised less than once a week. Interestingly, those who exercised less frequently were more likely to sleep for less than six hours, experience poor sleep quality, and receive a diagnosis for insomnia, sleep apnea, and restless leg syndrome [5].

Another survey involved adults aged 23 to 60 found that approximately 78% to 83% of individuals who engaged in light, moderate, or vigorous exercise reported "good" to "very good" sleep quality. They also tended to get more sleep than required during the work week. In contrast, the figure dropped to 56% for those who did not exercise [5].

But it's not only how long you sleep, but when you sleep. Another study discovered that individuals who exercised at 4:00 p.m. or later were more likely to fall asleep quickly, experience adequate deep sleep, and wake up feeling well-rested. Evening exercise also led to increased slow wave sleep and extended latency for rapid eye movement sleep compared to a control group [15]. It is worth noting, however, that those who exercise within an hour before sleep are likely to experience poorer sleep quality.

Given the diverse findings of these studies and the wide range of individual needs and goals, it's important to adapt your workout regimen and sleep schedule to suit your specific requirements and sleep patterns. By embracing this personalized approach, you can strike a harmonious balance between both your productivity and your progress towards your fitness goals.
Remember, the key lies in honoring your body's signals and adapting your regimen accordingly, paving the way for sustainable success and life-long health.

NICKI BRIGHT

WORK SMARTER, NOT HARDER

As a personal trainer, I've heard a wide array of unique fitness aspirations. From clients yearning for a perfectly sculpted "bubble butt" that could rival a Kardashian, to those seeking a back so chiseled it resembles the mighty ridges of the Appalachian Mountains. The fascinating range of goals and desires they bring to the gym inspires me to tailor their workouts to transform visions into tangible realities.

With that said, my approach has always been centered around establishing realistic and attainable goals. This entails delivering candid feedback and dispelling common misconceptions. I believe in the value of straightforward honesty, as it ultimately serves everyone's best interests.

When beginning a fitness journey, most people tend to focus on shedding pounds or achieving a lower number on the scale. However, what they may not realize is that the number on the scale doesn't tell the whole story. In fact, the opposite—gaining weight in the form of muscle—can have an unexpected outcome that will likely redefine their goals and ultimately, deepen their understanding of what it means to be healthy.

The words "weight gain" get a bad rap. Often misunderstood and unfairly stigmatized, most people think that gaining weight automatically equates to gaining fat. However, weight gain doesn't always have a negative effect on your physique. In fact, it can lead to an improvement in your physique.

Intentional weight gain is caused by the accumulation of lean muscle mass. This is known as hypertrophy, or the enlargement and strengthening of muscle fibers. Engaging in resistance training exercises stimulates the muscles to adapt and grow in response to the demands placed upon them. This is why after a few months of strength training and building a solid foundation of muscle, you may notice the number on the scale go up, not down.

The key in proper weight gain lies in gaining muscle and losing fat, a process known as "body recomposition," introduced in the previous chapter. Body recomposition is achieved by lifting weights and eating an adequate amount of calories. For beginners looking to gain muscle, that might mean a caloric surplus, but for more advanced lifters with a foundation of muscle already built, that might mean a caloric deficit. The difference between a surplus and deficit will be explained in chapter eight: The Basics of Nutrition.

For now, all you need to know is that the calories you eat during the day will go towards building up the muscle you broke down during your workout, rebuilding them to be stronger and more resilient. This demonstrates that the relationship between muscle repair and food energy is linked. By increasing your muscle mass, you effectively "boost" your body's metabolism, resulting in a higher caloric expenditure and facilitating fat loss.

This is why it's important to shift from focusing solely on the number on the scale to the composition of muscle gained. Embracing weight gain in the form of muscle is a game-changing state of mind, pushing you out of your comfort zone and challenging preconceived notions about fitness. While it may be uncomfortable at first, a mindset that embraces a higher number on the scale will allow you to find freedom with exercise and food, ultimately setting the stage for the best version of yourself.

The days of mindlessly pushing through grueling workouts with little consideration for technique or efficiency are gone. Instead, you will work smarter instead of harder by leveraging your time, energy, and resources to achieve the best possible outcomes. By adopting this approach, you'll discover that it's not just about the quantity of work you put in, but rather the quality of each repetition, set, and exercise.

MISCONCEPTION #1
BECOMING BULKY

Usually, when I tell women that they should be lifting weights, their face contorts to worry and confusion. They say, "But I don't want to become bulky."

First and foremost, lifting weights will not make women bulky. The fact of the matter is, women can't get as big as men can, unless they train extremely hard and follow a strict diet for a significant period. In order to achieve a male athlete's physique without the use of steroids, women would need to resort to taking steroids themselves.

This difference between men and women is primarily due to hormonal variances. Testosterone, a hormone that plays a pivotal role in muscle growth and size, is significantly more abundant in men. Research demonstrates that following intense strength-based exercise, testosterone levels in men can be up to ten times higher than in women [18]. Consequently, men find it easier to achieve a large, bulky appearance, while women would require a considerably greater amount of training and nutritional efforts to reach the same outcome.

2022
Lifting heavy with a portable weight set

If you previously followed a weightlifting routine and felt that you were becoming too bulky, there's a reason for that. But here's the secret: it wasn't the weightlifting. Instead, it's more likely that you were consuming an excessive amount of food.

It's no mystery that rigorous exercise increases hunger levels. This makes it easy to overeat if proper monitoring and adjustments are not made. Even though you are working out by lifting heavy weights and burning a lot of calories, eating too much will lead to unintended fat gain, or a feeling of bulkiness. In general, women who consume the appropriate amount of calories to maintain their weight, emphasize protein intake, and lift weights three to five times per week, can achieve a lean physique without resembling the stereotypical "bulky" look.

Instead, it's essential to adopt a balanced approach to achieve a lean and muscular physique. This involves combining a strength-focused workout program with a nutrition plan tailored to your individual needs.

It's important to dispel the myth that weightlifting will automatically make women bulky. With the understanding that women's hormonal composition and natural muscle-building capacity differ from men's, it becomes clear that achieving a lean, muscular physique requires a balanced approach of strength training and tailored nutrition.

By embracing weightlifting and adopting a nutrition plan that suits their unique needs, women can unlock their full potential and cultivate a strong, empowered, and healthy body without falling into the misconception of becoming overly bulky.

MISCONCEPTION #2
TONING

Motivated by the fear of excessive bulkiness, women go to great lengths in pursuit of their dream body. In their quest, they often become influenced by misguided notions and inaccurate advice. Unfortunately, a commonly misunderstood concept is "toning."

When women say they want to "tone," they are usually describing the image in their head of someone who is lean and muscular, but doesn't look like a professional bodybuilder. While that's likely an accurate description of the body they hope to achieve, it's important to understand that a "toned" look requires a decent amount of muscle mass.

Before anyone should even consider getting "toned," they must ask themselves how long they've been lifting heavy weights. If their answer is that they've either never lifted heavy or lift heavy for generally anything less than three to five years, the result in them losing weight will just be a smaller version of their current self or the dreaded "skinny-fat" physique. No amount of fat loss will make them look "toned" if they do not have enough muscle mass in the first place.

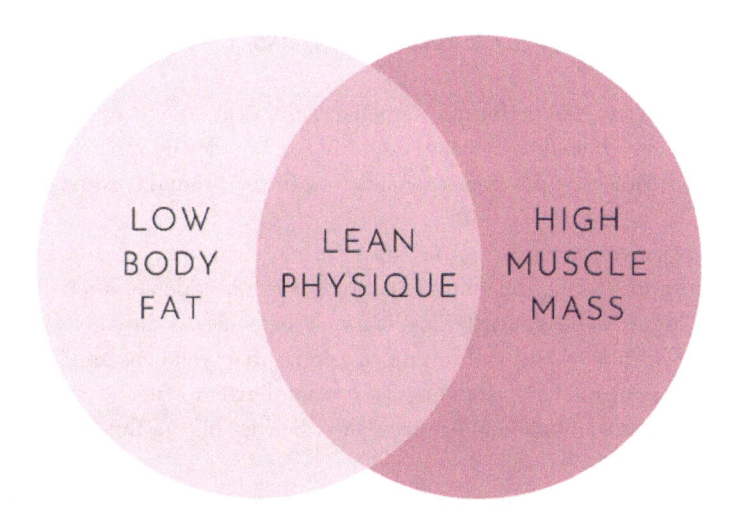

LOW BODY FAT — LEAN PHYSIQUE — HIGH MUSCLE MASS

In order to gain muscle, you must lift heavy weights and eat in a caloric surplus. Lifting light weights, Pilates, yoga, and resistance bands are not going to put on muscle mass nearly as fast or as effectively as lifting heavy weights will.

Lifting heavy means lifting weights that only allow you to do 12 reps until you fail. Failing means not being able to do another rep by quite literally failing to lift it. If you can do more than 12 reps with the selected weight and with proper form, increase the weight by 5-10% each set until you are around 12 reps from failure. As you continue, you will get stronger and will need to increase the weight gradually to keep your rep range around 12. Of course, there are other more advanced approaches to training, but this is a fool-proof way to make gains as a beginner.

Once muscle mass is established, the next step is to shred the fat around the muscle. This is done through carefully manipulating diet and lowering caloric intake (see chapter eight). Thus, by understanding this simple principle, the image of that toned, sculpted physique can become a reality.

MISCONCEPTION #3
SPOT REDUCING FAT

I used to believe that performing targeted exercises like crunches, clamshells, and arm circles would magically sculpt my abs, slim down my legs, and tone my arms. However, this mindset couldn't be further from the truth.

The idea that you can direct fat loss at a particular area on your body is called "spot reducing" fat and it's a common misconception promoted in the fitness industry. In reality, fat loss can only be achieved through a calorie deficit, which is when you burn more calories than you consume in a day (see chapter eight). Understanding this relationship between food energy and fat loss is a crucial step in maximizing the efficiency of your fitness pursuits.

Interestingly, by engaging in resistance exercises with the intention to slim down fatty areas, you may inadvertently make those areas appear larger rather than smaller. This is because the stress placed on your muscles during weightlifting causes them to adapt and grow, which can result in an increase in muscle size. Therefore, instead of reducing the size of the fatty areas, the muscles underneath become larger, creating an enlarged appearance. While it may be a hard pill to swallow, this reality highlights the importance of understanding the complexities of body composition and the limitations of spot reduction.

However, exercises like crunches and clamshells still serve a purpose. Building muscle provides numerous advantages when it comes to shedding fat, such as an improved metabolism and increased caloric expenditure. However, fat loss is a systemic process that occurs throughout the body rather than in specific targeted areas. Regardless of the frequency or intensity with which you target specific muscles, fat loss is not localized and cannot be isolated to one particular region.

Keep in mind that each person is unique, and the way bodies respond to fat loss can vary. For instance, a female may initially observe fat loss in areas such as the hips, butt, and thighs, while a male might notice it first in the upper body, such as the back and arms. The distribution of fat loss will differ based on individual factors and genetic predispositions.

Regardless of these tendencies, cultivating a lean physique requires a comprehensive approach that combines resistance training, cardiovascular exercise, and a balanced diet. By promoting overall fat loss and simultaneously building muscle, you can gradually transform your body composition and achieve a more proportionate and sculpted appearance.

MISCONCEPTION #4
IT'S ALL ABOUT THE SCALE

Frequently, when people are dissatisfied with their physical appearance, their immediate response is to focus on making the number on the scale go down. They embark on an exhausting path of restricting food intake and intensifying exercise, pushing themselves to their limits. This pattern is one I know all too well.

In theory, it seems logical that consuming fewer calories should result in less fat being stored. When the body is subjected to a significant calorie deficit, where the intake of calories is notably lower than the amount needed for proper functioning, it triggers a series of adaptive responses. In an effort to ensure its survival, the body goes into a state of heightened vigilance and becomes cautious about conserving energy.

During such circumstances, the body perceives a potential scarcity of fuel and reacts by slowing down its metabolic rate. It becomes more efficient at utilizing the limited calories it receives, prioritizing essential bodily functions. This adaptive mechanism aims to preserve energy stores and maintain vital bodily functions.

Furthermore, when the body is deprived of adequate fuel from dietary sources, it may resort to breaking down muscle tissue for energy. The loss of muscle mass can have negative consequences on overall body composition, strength, and metabolic rate.

As you are starting to notice, this ties in closely with the previous section regarding toning. You will not achieve a "toned" physique with no muscle mass. This is why there is so much misunderstanding between losing weight and losing body fat.

Weight loss refers to a reduction in total body weight, which comprises both fat and muscle. This ultimately leads to a lower number on the scale, but due to the loss of muscle mass, may not yield a desired physique outcome. As previously discussed in this chapter, achieving a low body weight with insufficient muscle mass can result in the undesirable "skinny-fat" look.

Instead of losing overall weight, the objective should be to lose only body fat while preserving and building upon existing muscle mass. Through a combination of weightlifting and manipulation of caloric intake, this balance can be achieved. The beauty of weightlifting lies within its ability to utilize the nutrients we consume to fortify our fatigued muscles.

Another important factor to keep in mind is that muscle is more dense than fat. In other words, muscle cells take up less space than fat cells. This means that losing body fat and increasing muscle mass will likely cause your weight to stay the same or even increase. Oftentimes, when people notice this, they get frightened. Blaming their failure to lose weight on their new exercise routine, they abandon it, when in reality, they are just beginning to see its positive impact.

Throughout my personal journey, weightlifting has led to a notable transformation in my physique. In order to do this, I needed to embrace weight gain as a part of this process. I managed to gain twenty-five pounds. Seeing the difference in the two photos below, you can see that gaining weight does not automatically equate to a worsened physique.

Left: 2018, 115 pounds
Right: 2022, 140 pounds

What makes the journey even more liberating is the freedom it grants you in your relationship with food. By nourishing your body adequately to support your training, you can comfortably indulge in sweet treats or other favorite foods every once in a while, without feelings of guilt or restriction.

The understanding that fat loss does not equate to weight loss will bring about a sense of balance and harmony. You will be able to embrace a healthier relationship with food, viewing it as a source of nourishment and enjoyment rather than a source of stress or deprivation. Weightlifting will not only sculpt your physique, but it will also transform your mindset and approach to nutrition.

Now that we have effectively debunked and dispelled numerous misconceptions about weightlifting, it's time to work smarter, not harder.

Armed with accurate knowledge and a clear understanding of the principles behind weightlifting, we can now explore the finer details that will allow you to optimize your efforts and maximize your results.

HYPERTROPHY AND ENDURANCE

Hypertrophy training and endurance training are two distinct forms of exercise that are commonly confused and misunderstood. While both types of training contribute to overall fitness, they target different physiological adaptations and have vastly different end results.

Hypertrophy training, also known as strength training or resistance training, focuses on increasing muscle size and strength. The primary objective of hypertrophy training is to stimulate muscle growth through the use of progressive overload, typically achieved by lifting heavy weights for a lower number of repetitions, between six to 12. This type of training is commonly associated with bodybuilding and is aimed at building a well-defined and aesthetically pleasing physique.

On the other hand, endurance training primarily aims to improve the body's ability to sustain prolonged physical activity. It involves activities that increase cardiovascular fitness and enhance the efficiency of the body's energy systems, enabling individuals to perform continuous, low-to-moderate intensity exercise for extended periods. The focus is on developing aerobic capacity, improving cardiovascular health, and increasing stamina.

Endurance training typically involves activities like long-distance running, cycling, swimming, or participating in endurance-based sports. If your goal is to excel in these sports, then training accordingly makes sense. But remember, although endurance training can stimulate some muscle growth, the degree at which hypertrophy happens typically less significant when compared to dedicated hypertrophy training.

It is worth noting that individuals who solely rely on endurance training, without incorporating hypertrophy-focused training, may experience weight loss. However, this weight loss entails a combination of both body fat and muscle mass. Intense activities associated with endurance training can lead to substantial calorie expenditure, and without sufficient caloric intake, muscle mass may be compromised. Consequently, for individuals striving to achieve a lean physique and genuine functional fitness, placing emphasis on muscle growth becomes crucial.

Despite their differences, the confusion between hypertrophy and endurance training can arise due to certain similarities. For instance, both types may involve weightlifting exercises, but the goals and methodologies differ. Some people may mistakenly believe that lifting lighter weights for higher repetitions will lead to muscle growth and endurance simultaneously, which is not entirely accurate.

By shifting the focus towards muscle development through incorporating hypertrophy training into their routine, you pave the way for a leaner, more sculpted physique while reaping the benefits of and functional strength.

NUTRITION IS PARAMOUNT

I've observed countless individuals over the years succumbing to the misconception that as long as they are physically active, they can disregard the importance of their dietary choices. It's surprising to discover that a significant portion of ultramarathon runners, despite regular exercise, are overweight. It took me a while to comprehend this phenomenon until I realized the significance of proper nutrition.

Here's the unexpected truth: 80% of changes in physique are influenced by diet, while the remaining 20% are attributed to exercise. Most people tend to overlook the quantity and quality of their food. Consequently, they find themselves bewildered and frustrated when they fail to lose fat and attain their desired physique.

Food has been stigmatized in society for its ability to rapidly transform our bodies, mostly in the undesired direction. This prevalent belief leads many people to blame their exercise routines for weight gain. They might think they're not running long enough, or they need to work out twice a day. They may even consider Pilates or yoga as potential solutions. Surely, it must be anything but the unhealthy substances they consume!

The notion that increasing the frequency or intensity of exercise is a reliable strategy for fat loss is flawed for several reasons. Firstly, engaging in physical activity tends to stimulate hunger, leading to increased food consumption. Consequently, individuals may end up eating more than they burn, resulting in weight gain instead of loss. This counterproductive effect can be disheartening for those striving to shed pounds.

Secondly, sustaining a high volume of exercise over the long term can be challenging and unsustainable for many individuals. Life's demands, such as work, family, and other responsibilities, can make it difficult to maintain a rigorous exercise routine consistently. Without the ability to sustain such high levels of activity, the anticipated progress may not be achieved.

Lastly, relying solely on cardio-based exercise and neglecting other aspects of a well-rounded fitness regimen can limit progress. While cardio exercises have their benefits, incorporating strength training and other forms of exercise will help build muscle, boost metabolism, and improve body composition. Focusing solely on cardio workouts may result in limited progress and an incomplete transformation.

You can now see how nutrition outweighs exercise when it comes to achieving desired physical changes. While exercise plays a crucial role in overall health and fitness, it's nutrition that ultimately determines our success. Therefore, prioritizing a balanced and nutrient-dense diet is paramount for reaching and maintaining any physique goal.

WEIGHT FLUCTUATIONS

The average person has a basal metabolic rate, or BMR, of 2000 calories, which are the calories required for basic physiological functions while at rest. These functions include breathing, circulating blood, regulating body temperature, and supporting organ functions.

In comparison, there are approximately 3,500 calories in a pound of body weight. This means that in order to gain one pound of fat overnight, you would have to consume 3,500 calories over your BMR in a single day, equating to 5,500 calories.

Realistically, it's unlikely that you would be able to consume such a significant caloric surplus in that short a period. Consequently, it's highly improbable that you have gained a pound of fat overnight.

When you notice daily fluctuations in your weight, it's important to consider the other factors at play. These fluctuations can be attributed to many reasons, such as temporary water retention from consuming excessive sodium, the presence of a substantial meal in your digestive system, or even how recently you went to the bathroom. In fact, it's not uncommon for weight to fluctuate by up to five pounds in a single day.

The same principle applies to weight loss. Clients often come to me excitedly after a week of following their workout program, exclaiming, "I've already lost five pounds!" However, as a personal trainer, it's my responsibility to educate them about the unreliability of day-to-day scale readings. The truth is it took considerable time for their bodies to reach their current state—probably many years. Therefore, it's important to set realistic expectations regarding the time required to reverse those changes.

Sustainable weight loss typically occurs at a rate of about one to two pounds per week. Rapid weight loss can jeopardize muscle mass, while slower progress simply means that achieving goals will take longer. By incorporating weightlifting into your routine while maintaining a caloric deficit, you can preserve muscle mass and ensure that the weight that's lost is primarily from fat. The rate of fat loss is heavily influenced by the magnitude of the caloric deficit and the effectiveness of your workout program.

So, the next time you step on the scale and find it higher by a few pounds, there's no need to panic. In reality, your body is likely going through normal weight fluctuations, which can be influenced by factors like water retention and digestion. Sometimes, a simple bowel movement can lead to a decrease in weight and alleviate any concerns.

Additionally, if you've been engaging in regular exercise and strength training, it's possible that you're gaining muscle mass. Since muscle is more compact and takes up less space than an equivalent weight of fat, it can create the illusion of greater weight or size. As a result, it's possible for your weight to increase as you build muscle and replace fat.

Due to the scale's inconsistent nature, we should not place trust in daily weigh-ins. Only then can we leave behind the emotional attachment that usually accompanies it and focus instead on more meaningful indicators of progress like body fat percentage and muscle mass. Prioritize long-term progress and the development of sustainable habits rather than getting caught up in the inevitable day-to-day fluctuations of the scale.

AUNT FLO

Staying consistent with a workout routine is especially difficult for us ladies. We all know how easy it is to be derailed from our goals when that time of the month comes around, also known as the visit from Aunt Flo. It's not uncommon to experience lethargy, mood swings, and oftentimes extreme pain during her visit, much like what you might experience from your actual aunt coming for a visit (just kidding, Aunt Shawna and Aunt Shameka).

When those symptoms occur, exercise can feel like the last thing we want to do. However, a deeper understanding of the menstrual cycle allows us to realize that avoiding physical activity is not always the answer.

The menstruation cycle begins with the monthly visit from Aunt Flo, in which the internal lining of the uterine wall is secreted. This lasts for about three to five days. Day one of her visit also marks the beginning of the follicular phase. This phase continues for around five to six days after the last day of your period. When your period is over, estrogen levels begin to gradually increase.

This leads us to the ovulation phase, which is when your body releases an egg. It is also the phase in which, if sperm is present, can lead to implantation and pregnancy. Ovulation occurs right around the midpoint of the menstrual cycle, close to day 14.

After ovulation, the luteal phase brings a storm of hormones. During this phase, progesterone enters the picture and brings many physiological symptoms along with it. This phase ends when progesterone levels peak, after which both progesterone and estrogen levels decrease. This signals to the brain to call Aunt Flo, and the cycle continues.

With this deeper understanding of the phases of the menstrual cycle—and a slightly offensive analogy to relatives visiting frequently—we are ready to dive into the physiological effects that these changes have on exercise performance.

The menstruation phase of the cycle may be uncomfortable due to bleeding, so listening to your body is important. Yet still, it's important to make an effort to complete your regularly scheduled workout. If needed, light impact exercises are recommended. Suggestions include walking, hiking, yoga, or low volume strength training.

When progesterone and estrogen are at lower levels than normal, it's common to feel lethargic and tired. However, avoiding exercise is not the solution to feeling better. In fact, it's quite the opposite. Exercising during your period will actually make you feel better, as it reduces premenstrual symptoms (PMS), like mood swings, fatigue, breast tenderness, bloating, cramps, headaches, food cravings, acne, and sleep disturbances. Exercise also increases endorphin release and enhances mood.

However, the best effect from exercising during your period is an increase in strength and power. One study found that during the first two weeks of the menstrual cycle, the participants experienced greater strength gains and power [6]. This can largely be attributed to the low levels of female hormones.

The follicular phase begins right when your hormones are at their lowest, so as they gradually increase, your energy levels do too. This phase is the most opportune time to work out with intensity. Take advantage of this time in your cycle and train hard. Suggestions include heavy lifting, HIIT (high intensity interval training), long runs, and powerlifting. The ovulation phase is another opportune time to work out, as your testosterone levels are at their highest, while estrogen remains high.

The luteal phase might be a good time to back off a little bit, as your body temperature typically rises. Because of this, your body might be more sensitive to exercising in hot or humid environments and your athletic performance may decline. Additionally, high progesterone levels increase your resting heart rate, making it feel as if you are working harder than usual.

It is also known that during this phase, progesterone may have a catabolic effect, which makes it harder to repair muscles when the hormone is present. Thus, the best exercises to do during this time are those that are less strenuous, like outdoor hikes, yoga, and stretching.

At the end of the day, we're all human. All we can do is tune in to the signals of our bodies and make the best of what we've got. By embracing this fundamental truth, we can rest assured that we're always giving our all, leaving no room for disappointment to creep in. It's a reminder to trust ourselves, to honor our unique journey, and to embrace the beauty of being imperfectly human.

05 GYM ANXIETY

FINDING FITNESS FREEDOM

Experiencing overwhelming anxiety upon entering a gym is a topic that hits close to home for me. After realizing the staggering truth that roughly 50% of people feel too intimidated to even step foot inside a gym, I felt compelled to delve deeper into this matter by dedicating a whole chapter to it.

Take a moment to truly grasp the significance of that statistic. 50% of individuals who have the intention of going to the gym choose to abstain out of fear of judgment from others. But that's not the only reason. Knowledge on how to use equipment, what to do, lack of confidence, and insecurities about physical appearance are all factors that contribute to anxiety in the gym.

I must admit that I have experienced these emotions countless times throughout my life. Even now, after years of exercising in public gyms, I still feel the occasionally wave of anxiety. However, I have learned that these feelings have a trend, as they typically arise when I lack a clear workout plan, have fallen out of my routine, or find myself in an unfamiliar environment.

With that said, my goal is not to tell you how to eliminate all anxiety from your life. I believe anxiety is a normal intrinsic reaction to foreign environments. But there's a fine line between letting something bother you and letting something control you. Instead, I plan to show you how to reduce feelings of anxiety in places where they are not necessary, like the gym.

First and foremost, it's crucial to establish a clear distinction between genuine anxiety and the inherent discomfort that accompanies personal growth, two emotions commonly confused. The gym is not intended to be a place of constant comfort. Rather, it serves as a platform for pushing beyond familiar boundaries and embracing new challenges, such as conquering a push-up or a pull-up. Consequently, it's expected to experience a certain level of nervousness or anticipation when stepping into a gym environment. However, that should never manifest as any form of paralyzing anxiety that hinders your ability to accomplish your goals.

I wrestled with persistent gym anxiety for a long time, regrettably neglecting to take proactive steps in addressing it. When I began to write about my personal journey of overcoming gym anxiety for this book, I realized that the process to finding confidence in the gym was more complex than I initially believed. It took considerable time and involved navigating through various challenges. To truly grasp the depths of my experiences and the transformation that awaited me, let's start from the very beginning.

When I was 14, my mom purchased gym memberships for the entire family. I had never been to a gym before, so I went a couple of times with my dad. He taught me the basics of how to lift weights, like how to bench press and curl a dumbbell. That was the first time I had ever been exposed to heavy weights, but it was obvious that I was not a fan. They were extremely heavy, and my muscles were weak. Every time my dad said we had another set to do, I groaned.

Thinking back on those first few days of experimenting in the gym, I can still recall the sense of awe I felt while watching the strong, confident women strut through the weight room. Their intimidating strength and superior presence were a result of their many years of commitment and dedication to their sport.

Naturally, my first emotion was envy. I wanted to be able to do push-ups and pull-ups as effortlessly as they did. I wanted their knowledge, their, confidence, and their pride. I wanted it all and I wanted it instantly. But thinking about the sheer amount of time and effort necessary to attain their level of physicality was overwhelming and quite frankly, suffocating.

My second emotion was anxiety. As they walked past me, years of experience under their belts, I flooded myself with self-deprecating thoughts. *You don't know what you are doing. You don't have a plan. Your weights are so light. Look what that girl's lifting. I could never do that.*

Suddenly, curling 10-pound dumbbells seemed pointless. Because I had no plan for the rest of my workout, I hid in the sanctuary of the sauna. As I sat alone, sweat dripping off my body and steam engulfing me in a comforting hug, I felt momentarily free from the crippling anxiety. Yet still, I couldn't shake the weight of my disappointment, heavier than any dumbbell I had ever lifted.

I knew that skipping workouts to hide in the sauna would mean zero fitness progress, but I was at the mercy of my anxiety. After failing to push through my comfort zone for two weeks, I simply gave up trying.

It wasn't until two years later that I once again stepped foot into the gym. This time, I was drawn by a recommendation to try out a new group fitness class called Les Mills BodyPump. Seizing the opportunity for some cherished mother-daughter bonding, my mom and I went to our first class together. Beyond the shared experience, she became my reliable anchor when I felt out of my element.

The class was simple yet challenging. Each class, the instructor would shout into her microphone, exclaiming with pride, "We do over 500 reps in one class!" It was an intense, 60-minute workout that engaged the entire body, and unlike weightlifting, it didn't provoke the same level of frustration within me. The weights used were lighter and more manageable. By the end of the workout, everyone in the room was dripping in sweat, our muscles utterly fatigued.

Over the next couple of days, I was still sore from our one and only BodyPump class. In my mind, sore muscles equated to bigger muscles, so I took it as a sign that I was making monumental fitness progress. Over time the safety of the enclosed group fitness room became comfortable; there was no need to feel self-conscious when I could quietly blend into a class of twenty.

During this time, I had hit a plateau in my running progress. Despite running nearly 20-30 miles each week, I couldn't seem to improve my race times. The persistent lack of progress had left me disheartened and questioning my abilities. To make matters worse, I grappled with the deep-seated insecurity about my skinny-fat physique, which added another layer of disappointment to my overall experience. The combination of struggling to reach my running goals and feeling self-conscious about my physical appearance created a burden that weighed heavily on my spirit.

Discovering BodyPump felt like stumbling upon the missing puzzle piece in my relentless pursuit of achieving my dream physique. With no better solution in sight, I believed that BodyPump alone held the key to the toned arms and sculpted six-pack abs that I so desperately desired.

So, what did I do? I went to every single BodyPump class that I had time for, which was at least one class every day. Sometimes, two classes in one day. Week after week, my commitment grew stronger, and I became a familiar face in the group fitness community. I found myself forming a bond with the instructors and diligently preparing my station before class, often securing the coveted first spot.

It's safe to say I was obsessed. The thing is, I believed that this level of obsession was necessary. I mistakenly believed that my goals required an excessive level of dedication, even if that became an unhealthy fixation.

After several months of following this regimen, I noticed only minimal physique changes. I was no longer getting sore after every class, so I took that as a sign that I needed to push harder. I increased my weekly mileage to 30-40 miles while balancing five to six body pump classes every week. At the same time, I was putting extremely meticulous care into my diet. Despite this significant investment of time and energy, the progress of my physique was not aligning with my expectations.

Looking back, I realize that my exercise regimen was flawed in that I was lifting too light of weight for too many repetitions. Additionally, I lifted the same weights every class, with no application of progressive overload which is increasing intensity over time. While I didn't realize this back then, my approach was ineffective in yielding my desired results in terms of muscle growth.

Moreover, my diet was far from nourishing and well-balanced. I had been consuming too little, depriving my body of essential nutrients, particularly protein, and failing to incorporate a diverse range of nutrients into my daily meals. These two factors combined to create a significant obstacle in my journey towards fitness freedom.

At the time, I thought I was giving it my all. Frustratingly, the body I wanted was still very far away, leaving me more bewildered and confused than ever.

Throughout a period of roughly four months, as I dedicated myself fully to BodyPump, I gradually became aware of the toll it was taking on both my mental and physical well-being. I experienced a constant state of exhaustion, with little to show for my efforts. It became apparent that the negative effects on my mental health outweighed the minimal physical results I achieved.

I realized that I would need a more sustainable approach in order to bring harmony between effort and reward. Since running was the only thing in my life that had yielded somewhat significant physique progress, I went back to running exclusively, leaving the gym behind once again. The next time I would touch a weight would be at the beginning of the Covid-19 pandemic. I began my weightlifting journey at home during a global quarantine. It was March of 2020 and gyms were across the country were closing their doors. However, I wasn't interested in joining a gym. For me, the pandemic became an unexpected blessing in disguise.

The paralyzing anxiety that plagued me in public gyms had extinguished my interest in challenging myself at things I was not good at. For years, I clung to the comfort of running, finding solace in its familiarity. It wasn't until I was in the safety of my own home that I felt brave enough to venture into a different realm of exercise.

In the privacy of my own backyard, there were no prying eyes to witness my journey. I picked up my weights, getting myself through each rep with determined grunts and groans. I pushed myself to the point of failure, even collapsing on the ground after completing my final set of push-ups from my knees. These solitary moments became my refuge, allowing me to push past my limitations and begin to shatter self-imposed barriers without the fear of judgment or scrutiny.

Throughout my fitness journey, I was determined to let absolutely nothing get in my way. I wasn't going to sacrifice my progress because of external factors, such as my environment or limited equipment. If the temperature was too hot outside, I'd take my equipment inside. If the dumbbells were too light, I'd strap more weights on with Velcro. Every challenge that was thrown at me, I found a solution to overcome it.

In order to get good at something, you first must become obsessed with it. So, while the rest of the world waited out the quarantine on cushioned sofas with their favorite reality TV show, I refused to wait for opportunities to come my way. Instead, I plunged headfirst into the world of weightlifting, driven by a thirst for knowledge and a burning desire to improve.

I devoured countless articles on muscle building, meticulously selecting social media accounts that provided education on proper exercise form and technique. I immersed myself in a world of learning, ensuring that every glance, every click, and every scroll added to my understanding and expertise. There was no shortage of motivation when knowledge surrounded me, constantly fueling my desire to be better.

To my surprise, I quickly outgrew the light dumbbells and minimal home gym equipment. Once the lockdown was over, I joined a public gym so I could have access to heavier weights. Little did I anticipate the impact that simple decision would have on my strength and potential.

Having built a solid foundation of strength and knowledge over the past six months in my backyard, I was confident in my physical abilities. I knew which machines to use, and I knew exactly which weights I was ready for. The transition to a public gym felt natural and I quickly began to prefer it over the home gym.

As I looked back on my early gym experiences with my dad, nearly five years ago, I came to a realization about the unwarranted self-consciousness that had plagued me. In those initial days, I was preoccupied with thoughts of judgment from others, scrutinizing my every move and constantly comparing myself to those around me. However, with the passage of time and a deeper understanding that results require patience and dedication, I could now see the futility of those concerns.

I recognized that every individual's fitness journey is unique, and no two paths will be identical. Instead of fixating on what others might think or achieve, I came to understand the significance of focusing solely on my own progress and growth. Embracing this newfound perspective, I had freed myself from the shackles of self-doubt and comparison. I learned to cherish the small victories, celebrate my personal milestones, and revel in the joy of my unique journey. In doing so, I unlocked a deeper sense of self-assurance and finally found myself free from worry.

I attribute most of my success with finding this freedom to spending time learning in the non-judgmental comfort of my home. There, I was able to experiment and learn, without a single ounce of concern about what anyone else was thinking about me. Only then was I truly able to immerse myself in the joy and benefits of weightlifting.

I will never forget the extreme embarrassment and self-loathing I would feel when I struggled to complete even a single push-up. Yet now, able to do one-hundred push-ups in ten minutes, I had forged an unwavering conviction that with diligent effort, there were no limits to what I could achieve.

Yet still, there have been occasions where lingering gazes or unwarranted stares have made me feel uncomfortable in the gym. In such moments, I've come to realize that I have two choices. I can choose to disregard their actions, recognizing that there's a slim possibility they intended any harm. Or I can take the proactive approach of addressing the situation directly and expressing my discomfort.

Having experimented with both approaches, and if the other person is making me seriously uncomfortable, I've discovered that the most effective way to handle these situations is by approaching the individual and initiating a friendly introduction. Oftentimes, it's just a misunderstanding. Surprisingly, this approach has led to the formation of several new friendships.

Regardless of who's watching, the gym is a place where I go to work on myself. I put my head down, turn my music on, and get to work. I don't waste time worrying about what anyone else is doing, because I already have too much to focus on—how many sets I'm doing, what rep I'm on, and what exercise is next.

Feeling confident in the gym is something that requires continual work. I find that if I take a vacation or a break from the gym, I feel more anxiety when I come back. Typically, comfort is quick to build itself back up after a few days of consistency. This is another reason why consistency in a workout program is so crucial.

While my battle with gym anxiety had a happy ending, not everyone needs to go through what I did. Having accumulated a wealth of experience in both my personal training journey and working with clients, I've discovered valuable insights on how to navigate and overcome anxiety in the gym.

Building confidence in the gym doesn't necessitate starting at home with a personal gym setup. My journey may have taken that route, but everyone's path is distinct and should be embraced as such. If creating a home gym aligns with your circumstances, by all means, go for it. However, I not everyone has the means or space for such an arrangement.

With this understanding in mind, I have compiled seven valuable tips that I've gathered from countless hours of observation and personal experimentation. Embracing these strategies, you can avoid unnecessary anxiety or alleviate any concerns that might hinder your progress.

Remember, the gym can be an empowering space where you can flourish and grow, irrespective of your starting point or background. Embrace your uniqueness, explore what works best for you, and let these tried-and-true tips guide you toward a fulfilling and rewarding fitness journey.

TIP #1
MAKE A PLAN

Having a written plan for the gym is essential for anyone serious about their fitness journey. It serves as a roadmap that provides clarity on your goals and outlines the steps required in order to achieve them.

By putting your intentions on paper, you create a sense of accountability that motivates you to stay committed to your workout routines. It becomes a constant reminder of why you started and what you're working towards, keeping you inspired and focused on your fitness journey. So, whether you're a beginner or a seasoned gym-goer, having a well-designed plan is essential for making the most out of your fitness journey.

To create an effective plan, start by posing these five fundamental questions. Jot them down on paper or on your phone for easy reference. Here are several examples of questions you should ask yourself to begin formulating your plan.

What is the main objective I aim to accomplish?
Example: *Lose 20 pounds so I can fit into my favorite dress.*

How many workout days per week are necessary to reach this goal?
Example: *A plan of three strength training workouts and two cardio sessions each week will help me maintain my caloric deficit and build muscle definition (more about this in The Basics of Nutrition chapter).*

What should my diet entail to achieve this goal?
Example: *A weight loss goal requires a caloric deficit, so I will aim for a deficit of about 300-500 calories each day (more about this in The Basics of Nutrition chapter).*

What is the estimated timeline for achieving this goal?
Example: *At a rate of one pound lost each week, I can realistically achieve my goal in four to five months.*

What is the primary obstacle hindering me from attaining this goal?
Example: *I commonly resort to fast food for meals when I am on the road, so I plan to spend an hour or two on the weekend to prepare meals for the week.*

At this point, your objective is not to create the perfect plan, it's to simply put into words an initial plan that can—and should—be adjusted as your knowledge, goals and timeline evolve.

Once you have your initial answers, the next step is to construct a weekly schedule that incorporates various elements, such as workouts, work hours, lunch breaks, and social commitments. Tailor your schedule to include what you feel is necessary for your success.

Next, you must ask yourself, "Is this truly attainable for me?" If the answer is no, don't hesitate to make modifications. Setting realistic goals is crucial to avoid feelings of failure and maintain a positive and motivated mindset throughout your journey. When goals are unrealistic or overly ambitious, it becomes challenging to achieve them, leading to frustration and disappointment.

This is because oftentimes people to become overly fixated on the final destination, such as losing 20 pounds or being able to do 10 pull-ups, without truly understanding the immense amount of time and hard work that is required to achieve such significant goals. This is where it becomes clear that setting smaller milestones along the way is a more reliable way to ensure steady progress towards the ultimate objective, such as losing two pounds in two weeks, or being able to complete three pull-ups in a row by the end of the month.

Amidst all this planning, remember to find enjoyment in the day-to-day tasks, whether it's your invigorating morning workout or savoring an afternoon smoothie. Learn to adapt to the ebb and flow of life, because it's unpredictable and circumstances may change. However, with a well-structured plan, you can make adjustments and modifications without losing sight of your objectives. Embrace the process, knowing that with every session, you are steadily progressing towards your ultimate goal.

TIP #2
ADD IT TO THE CALENDAR

I always say, "Schedule your workouts like you schedule your work meetings." When you do this, you treat your fitness goals with the same level of importance as all the other essential tasks and activities in your life. Having workouts scheduled on your calendar, whether on your phone or on the wall, is a game-changer when it comes to staying organized and prioritizing your commitments.

Scheduling your workouts with this level of importance also plays a significant role in fostering a strong sense of accountability. When you allocate a specific time and date for your exercise routine, you create a commitment to yourself and your health. This commitment serves as a powerful motivator to follow through with your workouts, even on days when you might feel less enthusiastic.

This accountability that comes with scheduling workouts is crucial for maintaining consistency in your fitness journey. By sticking to a set workout schedule, you establish a reliable routine that becomes an integral part of your lifestyle.

Take a moment to sit down and organize your calendar, finding the best, consistent time in your daily routine to allocate for your workouts. Consider blocking out 60-90 minutes for each session, allowing for any necessary preparations such as travel, changing clothes, and personal needs. By setting aside this designated time, you eliminate the guesswork and create a clear plan for your exercise regimen.

By incorporating workouts into your calendar like this, you are able to visually plan the rest of your day around them. You can easily arrange other commitments, responsibilities, and activities to ensure they don't interfere with your exercise sessions. This proactive approach reduces the chances of feeling rushed or stressed during workouts, giving you the freedom to fully focus on each session. As a result, you can immerse yourself in the experience, enjoy the process, and reap all the physical and mental benefits of your workouts.

Scheduled workouts provide the framework for a consistent and balanced fitness routine. By adding them to the calendar, you set yourself up for success, making it easier to prioritize your health and fitness goals while fostering a positive and enjoyable exercise experience.

TIP #3
DO YOUR RESEARCH

To truly become the best version of yourself, it requires more than just wishful thinking and idle aspirations. It demands unwavering commitment and determination. It means consistently showing up, putting in the effort, and pushing through challenges, even when the path seems daunting and unknown.

Remember, everyone who is great was once a beginner. No one knows what they are doing when they start. In fact, many aspects of strength training are probably unfamiliar to you, such as how to position your arm during an overhead press or why you need to brace your core while performing squats. These are all things that take practice, repetition, and time to learn.

Instead of feeling discouraged or disheartened by the things you don't know, recognize that there is power that comes with being inexperienced. Inexperience implies a lack of knowledge or skill in a particular area, but it also signifies untapped potential and limitless opportunities for growth.

There's no doubt that at some point during your journey, you'll need guidance. When this happens, you must fight for your dreams by taking advantage of all resources available to you. There are countless reputable websites, blogs, and forums that offer valuable information and practical tips. Immerse yourself in educational books like this one, authored by experienced professionals, and don't underestimate the power of interpersonal connections. Engage with other gym enthusiasts, trainers, and fitness communities; exchange ideas, seek advice, and share experiences.

Embrace the journey of learning, for each step forward, no matter how small, will bring you closer to your goals. Every bit of knowledge gained, every skill developed, and every experience encountered contributes to your personal growth. By adopting a mindset of continuous learning and embracing the inherent power of inexperience, you open doors to a world of unimaginable possibilities.

Be relentless in your pursuit of growth and never settle for mediocrity. It's not going to be easy, but always remember, an investment in yourself pays the best dividends.

TIP #4
GET A GYM BUDDY

Knowing that someone else is relying on you to show up at the gym and give your best effort adds a level of responsibility and commitment that goes beyond just yourself. When you have a partner, skipping a workout not only means letting yourself down, but also disappointing your friend who is counting on you for support and companionship on their fitness journey.

The presence of a friend can provide reassurance and comfort, making the gym environment feel less intimidating and more welcoming. Knowing that you have a companion by your side who shares your goals and experiences can boost your confidence and help you navigate any uncertainties.

A friend can also be an incredible source of support, encouragement, and camaraderie. They can push you to challenge yourself, try new exercises, or increase your weights, all while providing a supportive and motivating environment. Exercising together can foster a sense of community and fun, turning the gym into a positive and uplifting environment. Having someone to chat with and share the journey with can distract from any anxious thoughts and help you focus on the enjoyable aspects of your workout.

Additionally, your friend might have different experiences, skills, or areas of expertise that they can share with you. You can learn from each other, exchange tips, and even try out new workout routines or techniques together. Having someone by your side who understands your fitness goals and shares your passion for health and wellness creates a sense of community and shared purpose that can make your workouts more enjoyable and effective.

If none of your friends or family members want to join you for a workout, don't worry. The gym offers a fantastic opportunity to meet people who share similar aspirations and are driven towards common goals. Approaching someone at the gym can be as simple as striking up a conversation by asking about their workout routine or how long they've been exercising. Complimenting their physique or form, if it feels appropriate, can also be a friendly icebreaker.

Oftentimes, friendships formed at the gym become an integral part of your daily routine. Embrace the chance to connect with like-minded people and cultivate lasting relationships within the gym community.

TIP #5
DRESS FOR SUCCESS

Wearing an outfit that boosts your confidence may play a bigger role in your workout than you might think. Whether it's those leggings that hug your legs perfectly or that tank top that is just the perfect shade of pink or even your favorite oversized sweater, the right attire can make you feel more positive and comfortable in any situation, including at the gym.

If none of your clothes excite you, it might be time to change that. Yes, I'm giving you permission to take a trip to the mall or online boutique and get yourself some new activewear. The anticipation of wearing your new outfit will likely increase your enthusiasm for starting your workout routine. Thus, consider your shopping spree and investment in yourself and your goals.

Although I'll admit, it's not the most frugal solution to finding motivation, the psychology of this trick has serious merit. When you feel good about your appearance, it translates into feeling more positive about your abilities and potential for progress. Moreover, a flattering outfit can improve your body image. It allows you to appreciate and embrace your unique physique, which in turn promotes a healthier relationship with exercise and a greater sense of self-acceptance.

Beyond the psychological benefits, having the right fabric, fit, and design can provide freedom of movement, proper support, and breathability, enabling you to perform exercises with ease and efficiency. When your workout gear fits well and allows for ease of movement, you can focus more on your exercises and less on any potential discomfort or distractions. Feeling physically comfortable can positively impact your mental state and reduce anxiety.

Remember that the most important thing is to feel comfortable and confident in what you're wearing, allowing you to focus on your fitness journey and reap the benefits of your hard work.

TIP #6
EMBRACE YOUR INDIVIDUALITY

Growing up, I was surrounded by fit, beautiful bodies, from social media to the magazines in the check-out aisle. Looking at my reflection in the mirror, I asked myself, *how were they able to look so much better than me?*

After years of diligently following an exercise regimen and achieving results that paled in comparison to theirs, it seemed obvious that they were doing something that I wasn't. Desperate to achieve their physique, I replicated their actions precisely, expecting that I would eventually sculpt a body identical to theirs. However, when that didn't happen, I was left even more frustrated and disappointed than ever.

In my desperation, I overlooked a fundamental aspect of human nature: our individuality. I failed to see that even if I did everything they did, I would never look exactly like them. Even if I was to copy their every workout and eat exactly what they ate, my physique would still look vastly different from theirs. This is because each person possesses a distinct genetic makeup that influences their body shape, muscle distribution, metabolism, and overall physical attributes.

Since each person has their own unique genetic makeup, we each have our own starting point. If we constantly measure ourselves against someone else's progress or appearance, we risk undermining our self-confidence and motivation. Some people may naturally have a higher propensity for muscle development, while others may have a faster metabolism or different fat distribution patterns. Factors such as bone structure, muscle fiber composition, and fat distribution cannot be altered solely through replication of external practices.

Instead of fixating on what we can't control, we must shift our focus to the things we can control, like consistent training, proper nutrition, and maintaining a healthy lifestyle.

Success in fitness is not about achieving an exact replica of someone else's body. It's about becoming the healthiest, strongest, and happiest version of ourselves.

TIP #7
THE BIG PICTURE

It's no secret that humans tend to be self-absorbed. While you may constantly think about your actions, appearance, and the opinions of others, you must recognize that the very people you are concerned about are likely scrutinizing themselves in the same way. In fact, they are probably too preoccupied with their own concerns to give any thought about you or what you are doing.

Our self-perception tends to be skewed, likely influenced by factors such as societal pressures, media images, and personal expectations. In other words, we are our own worst critics. This causes us to magnify perceived flaws and place undue importance on them, neglecting the broader picture of our overall well-being and unique attributes that make us who we are.

The truth is the aspects of our appearance that we agonize over may go largely unnoticed by others. People tend to focus more on the big picture of who we are rather than fixating on isolated physical details. By recognizing this tendency and letting go of the worry and self-criticism, we can foster a healthier relationship with our bodies and nurture self-acceptance.

By applying these seven tips, you take control of your fitness journey, no longer limited by self-doubt or societal expectations. Instead, you can explore, experiment, and discover what truly works best for you.

Through finding fitness freedom, you embrace challenges as opportunities for growth and see setbacks as stepping stones towards progress. This newfound sense of control over your body and mind becomes the driving force that propels you forward, transforming you into a healthier, stronger, and more fulfilled version of yourself.

ESTABLISHING DISCIPLINE

Think about motivation as a passing breeze on a hot summer day. It comes and goes, sometimes gently nudging you forward, but often fleeting and unpredictable. It can give you a momentary burst of energy and excitement, like a gust of wind that lifts your spirits. But just as quickly as it arrives, it can vanish, leaving you feeling stagnant and stuck.

On the other hand, discipline is like the steady flow of a river, continuously moving forward with purpose and determination. It doesn't rely on fleeting moments of inspiration, but instead relies on consistent effort and commitment. While motivation may come and go like a passing breeze, discipline is the flowing river, guiding you steadily towards your goals.

Discipline is built on the foundation of consistent habits, much like brushing your teeth in the morning or feeding your pets after dinner. It becomes an integral part of your routine, empowering you to take action and stay committed to your path. Embracing discipline over fleeting motivation is the key to achieving lasting success in your fitness journey and beyond.

At first, establishing discipline can be challenging, as it requires conscious effort and dedication. Yet, this investment pays off exponentially, sparing you the frustration of grappling with erratic motivation and frequent setbacks. Cultivating discipline from the start sets you on a path of self-empowerment and achievement.

To embark on the road to discipline, you can employ tricks to trick your mind into doing the challenging tasks. These strategies may take time and effort, but they will ultimately strengthen your resolve and resilience. Over time, you will no longer require such tricks, as your body will naturally adapt. But starting off on the right foot and with the proper mindset is crucial to making any sort of long-term fitness goal a reality.

BABY STEPS

In the pursuit of fitness goals, maintaining consistency in our workouts can be a formidable challenge. Life's demands, fatigue, and lack of motivation can easily throw us off track. However, it is during these moments that the strength of our discipline truly shines.

FINDING FITNESS FREEDOM

During a recent conversation with a client who had missed a workout, we discussed the importance of understanding the reasons behind the lack of motivation. We then worked on strategies to overcome these challenges and stay consistent. She explained, "I really wanted to go to the gym, but I felt exhausted on Wednesday due to a sleepless night and a busy day."

I reassured her, saying, "That's okay. Let's figure out why it happened and find ways to address it. Prioritizing good sleep and proper fueling can help. But remember, everyone has off days. The key is building discipline to push through these tough moments."

When it comes to implementing the concept of discipline and overcoming lack of motivation, practical strategies can make all the difference. In the case of my client, while she understood the idea, putting it into practice seemed daunting. To tackle this, we developed a simple, yet effective plan.

The plan involved mimicking the usual routine of heading to the gym, even on days when motivation was low. She would start by getting ready just like any other workout day, dressing in her gym clothes, fixing her hair, and putting on her workout shoes, breaking it down into baby steps. Then, she would get in her car and drive to the gym, without any pressure to go inside or start the workout immediately. In fact, she could turn around and go home if she wanted to, but the trick was that once she reached the gym, she usually found herself stepping out of the car and starting her workout. This technique proved effective, and the following week, she successfully completed all her scheduled workouts, using this strategy whenever she faced challenges.

When faced with low motivation or daunting obstacles, the thought of engaging in a full workout may feel overwhelming. However, by adopting this step-by-step approach, you can create a sense of ease and flexibility that empowers you to take action. Start by simply lacing your shoes, a seemingly insignificant task, but one that signals your intention to begin. Next, put on your workout clothes, mentally preparing yourself for the physical activity ahead. Grab your keys, a tangible action that reinforces your decision to head to the gym. As you get in the car, you are further solidifying your commitment.

Once you arrive at the gym, allow yourself the freedom to reassess. If you're still feeling uncertain or low on energy, you can choose to do some stretches or do a lighter workout instead. This incremental approach helps build momentum, transforming what might have initially felt like an insurmountable task into a series of manageable actions.

Allowing the flexibility to adapt based on your current state of mind and body, using "baby steps" provides a gentle entry point that often leads to long-term discipline.

ONE IS BETTER THAN NONE

On those particularly draining days when exhaustion and lack of motivation threaten to derail your workout plans, I have another simple, yet effective trick that has proven successful for myself and others time and time again. I call it the "one is better than none" approach.

This strategy builds upon the "baby steps" strategy by acknowledging that even a small step forward is infinitely better than standing still. When faced with the temptation to skip your workout, a four-mile run for example, the key is to commit to just one mile. Lace up your workout shoes, step outside, and tell yourself that you'll run that solitary mile, no matter what.

Surprisingly, that initial mile acts as a catalyst, propelling you to push beyond your initial intentions. Energized by the accomplishment of that first mile, you may find yourself eager to continue and complete your intended distance or even go beyond it.

When feeling unmotivated for weightlifting sessions, aim to complete a portion of your workout, or at a lower intensity. When you do this, the psychological barrier of fatigue will crumble, replaced by a newfound momentum and a sense of accomplishment that fuels your desire to push further.

Consistently practicing this strategy helps foster mental toughness, which is equally as vital as physical strength in your fitness journey. Mental toughness enables you to push through difficult moments and stay committed to your goals, even when faced with challenges or obstacles. It instills a mindset of resilience and determination, allowing you to maintain focus and stay on track, even when motivation wanes.

Remember that every workout doesn't need to be at maximum intensity or duration. The key is to keep moving forward, even if it means taking smaller steps on certain days. Embrace the power of incremental progress, and you'll find yourself consistently pushing past barriers, breaking through plateaus, and achieving new levels of strength and success in your fitness journey.

FIND ENJOYMENT

Discovering what ignites your excitement for exercise is a crucial step towards becoming disciplined. It's the little things, like your morning pre-workout coffee or a sunset run on the beach that can make a big difference.

Consider the elements that bring you joy, whether it's wearing your favorite pair of sneakers, finding a picturesque location for your workout, partnering up with a friend, or simply dedicating some time for yourself to find inner peace through breathing and meditation. It could also be the exhilarating sensation of exertion, the beads of sweat trickling down your body, or the rush of heat that flushes your face.

When you discover something that truly excites you during your workouts, hold on to it tightly. Use it as your reliable tool, for the source of your excitement can rekindle a spark of determination within you and help push past the obstacles.

Personally, I find solace in immersing myself in heart-thumping, pulse-pounding music, which sets the stage for an adrenaline-fueled workout. Even on days when motivation is fleeting, the mere thought of listening to my favorite high-energy songs while lifting heavy weights fills me with such excitement that I can hardly wait to start my workout.

Your unique reason to enjoy exercise serves as a reminder of the joy and fulfillment that waits for you on the other side of your workout, making the journey more enticing and worthwhile. Embracing and leveraging these personal motivators will propel you forward through the monotony of everyday tasks.

FORGIVE AND FORGET

When beginning a fitness journey, people typically have a vision of what they want to achieve, whether that's a more fit body or a more balanced lifestyle. During these initial stages, motivation is at its peak, and people set ambitious and lofty expectations for themselves. The excitement and determination to make positive changes drives them forward.

However, as the journey progresses, challenges may arise. Life's demands, unforeseen obstacles, or fluctuations in motivation can make it difficult to maintain the level of consistency required to meet those high expectations. When they fall short of their goals, it can be disheartening and dispiriting. The weight of disappointment can take a toll on their spirit, potentially derailing their progress.

In such moments, it's not uncommon for people to feel like they've failed and lead them to question whether their fitness journey is worth continuing. Feelings of frustration, guilt, and self-criticism may emerge, pushing them towards the brink of giving up entirely. But the problem does not lie in their effort or your determination; the problem lies in the nature of the goal itself.

Setting goals that demand 100% consistency and perfection is like setting yourself up for failure. Life is unpredictable, and striving for absolute perfection is unrealistic. One missed workout or one indulgent meal does not define overall progress. Instead, adopt a "forgive and forget" mindset and view setbacks as temporary obstacles rather than reasons to give up.

By setting realistic, achievable goals, you foster a more sustainable and positive approach to fitness, where occasional deviations are acknowledged and accepted without self-judgment. In this way, you build resilience by focusing on long-term goals rather than short-term failures.

SUPPORT SYSTEM

Establishing a support system, such as workout buddies or accountability partners, can provide encouragement and help maintain consistency. These friends can provide motivation, share experiences, and offer support during challenging times, making it easier to stay on track and avoid the negative spiral of thoughts and behaviors.

Joining the Wednesday Night Run Club marked a momentous turning point in my life. I went from not believing I could run one mile to running 50-mile ultramarathons. The respect I developed for my fellow runners became a source of motivation and their accomplishments became a shining example of what was possible. Hearing their stories instilled in me a belief that I, too, possessed the strength and resilience to push beyond my perceived limitations.

During challenging times, such as moments of self-doubt or setbacks, working out with friends or running with a group acted as my safety net, offering reassurance, guidance, and the perspective needed to stay on track. The sharing of experiences and advice broadened my horizons, expanded possibilities, and helped me break through mental barriers.

Whether it's through friendly competition, shared milestones, or the simple act of cheering each other on, a support system provides the necessary fuel to sustain motivation and maintain consistency on the fitness journey, ultimately leading to greater long-term success. Seek out fitness clubs, online forums, or whatever you have access to in your community.

Immerse yourself in the fitness landscape and you might just ignite a revitalized source of motivation and determination within you. Building a strong support system will help you stay committed, overcome obstacles, and reach your fitness goals with greater confidence and joy.

REMEMBER YOUR "WHY"

Another effective approach to establish discipline is to clarify your goals. Take time to reflect on why you started in the first place and what you hope to achieve. By reconnecting with your deeper purpose and the reasons behind your aspirations, you can reignite your determination.

One powerful way to do this is to write your goals down. Putting your aspirations on paper not only gives them a tangible form, but also allows you to clarify and organize your thoughts. As you write, take the opportunity to be specific and detailed about what you want to accomplish. Whether it's improving your endurance, losing weight, building strength, or participating in an athletic event, articulate your goals clearly and specifically. For example:

Goal: *Lose 15 pounds*
Exercise: *Dedicate three days per week to going to the gym, with an emphasis on building lower body strength*
Nutrition: *Eat in a caloric deficit consistently while making sure I get a large serving of protein in each meal*
Duration: *In a caloric deficit of about 300-500 calories each day, I should expect to lose 15 pounds in five to six months.*

Visualization is another essential tool in this process. Once you have written down your goals, take the time to visualize the outcomes you desire. Create a vivid mental image of yourself achieving those goals, envisioning how it will feel, how you will look, and the positive impact it will have on your life. This practice helps create a strong emotional connection to your aspirations, making them more compelling and inspiring.

By engaging in this goal setting and visualization process, you are creating a framework for success. It allows you to align your actions and efforts with your deepest desires and motivations. When faced with challenges or moments of wavering motivation, you can revisit your written goals and tap into the mental images you have created. They serve as a constant reminder of what you are striving for and reinforce your commitment to your fitness journey.

As you make progress and achieve milestones, celebrate those accomplishments and set new goals to keep the momentum going. This ongoing reflection and adjustment of your goals will help you stay engaged and continue pushing yourself towards new heights.

FINDING FITNESS FREEDOM

Within the broad scope of fitness, the road to triumph will be a wild rollercoaster ride of challenges and choices. Nobody will maintain consistency and discipline at a perfect 100% all the time. There will be missed workouts, occasions of subpar performance, and days of consuming too much or too little food. Life is unpredictable and setbacks will happen.

However, getting off track every once in a while does not define someone as a failure, and it certainly doesn't justify giving up. Instead, when these setbacks happen, accept that you are human and it is in our nature to make mistakes. When you fall off, admit that you made a bad decision and make the intention to get back on track as soon as you can. Remember: fitness is not meant to diminish the quality of your life; it's meant to enhance it. Being fit can make everyday activities more enjoyable, rewarding, and fulfilling.

However, if you find yourself dreading your workouts, sacrificing time with loved ones, or absolutely hating the process, it might be a sign that you need to change your routine. While it's true that some situations require periods of more discipline than others, it's imperative that you strike a balance between enjoyment of life's pleasures and achieving your fitness goals. This balance is vital because an unsustainable routine is unlikely to be maintained in the long run, rendering your fitness journey as no more than a fleeting moment on the page of your life.

Picture this: you stand at a crossroads, where two paths diverge—one leads to the land of fitness, a place of sweat, discipline, exhilaration, and transformation, while the other winds its way to the realm of fat, a land of comfort, indulgence, and stagnant growth.

The catch is, both paths are strewn with obstacles, whether that's consistency with your workouts or grappling with feeling disappointed in your body and its abilities. Both paths require discomfort and struggle, but here's the kicker: if you dare to venture down the fitness path, a marvelous transformation awaits, one that embodies strength, well-being, and self-confidence. The choice is yours.

07
THE SIX FUNDAMENTAL EXERCISES

The six fundamental exercises are exercises that everyone should practice because they simulate movements you do in everyday life. They are also known as "compound" exercises because they engage more than one muscle group.

The significance of these fundamental exercises lies not only in their ability to engage multiple muscle groups, but also in the demand they place on proper technique, focus, and intention. To reap their full benefits, it is crucial to perform these exercises with precision, paying close attention to form and execution. In doing so, we maximize the effectiveness of each movement and minimize the risk of injury.

Employing the six fundamental exercises in a workout program means embracing a holistic approach to fitness, where strength, coordination, and stability work together harmoniously. These exercises serve as a solid foundation for building a well-rounded physique and developing the physical capabilities necessary for everyday activities.

However, before we dive into the fundamental exercises, we will first go over the basic aspects of weightlifting. By understanding these principles, you'll not only enhance your performance and maximize results, but also reduce the risk of injuries and ensure a safe and effective training experience.

MINDSET

Weightlifting, in its essence, is meditation. When you enter the weight room, you leave everything else behind, including stress, concerns, or worries. It's a space where you detach yourself from the hustle and bustle of the world and allow yourself to fully immerse in the present moment. This perspective sets the stage for a successful and productive lifting session.

Weightlifting requires a mind-muscle connection, in which you mentally visualize the muscle you are engaging while executing the exercise. The mind-muscle connection in weightlifting is so crucial that it can quite literally make or break your lift.

This concept was demonstrated in a study conducted by researchers at the University of Maryland in their examination of the effects of mental imagery on muscle strength. In the study, participants were divided into two groups: one group performed physical practice of a specific exercise, and the other group practiced mental imagery while performing the same exercise. The researchers measured the participants' muscle strength before and after the interventions.

The results were astonishing. Both groups demonstrated improvements in muscle strength, however the mental imagery group displayed significantly more gains in strength, comparable to those achieved solely through physical practice. This clear evidence establishes the crucial role of the mind-muscle connection in maximizing the efficiency and efficacy of workouts [14].

Similar to meditation, your breathing pattern plays a crucial role in your lifting sessions, as well. This means to practice breathing in on the eccentric movement (the part of the exercise where your muscles are being lengthened) and breathing out on the concentric movement (the part of the exercise where your muscles are being contracted).

For example, you breathe out as you bicep curl a dumbbell towards your chest. You breathe in as you let the weight fall back down to your side. Syncing your breath with the movement in this way will help you maintain control, stability, and proper form.

This conscious breathing technique also has a psychological aspect. The rhythmic and deliberate flow of breath provides a focal point for your concentration, enhancing your mind-muscle connection and focus during the lift. It helps you stay grounded, present, and in tune with your body, allowing for a more intentional execution of the exercise.

Incorporating the mind-muscle connection and synchronized breathing into your weightlifting routine not only enhances your physical performance, but also deepens your connection with your body. This meditative state allows you to push beyond previous limits and tap into your peak performance.

REST TIME

Resting the appropriate amount of time between sets is a crucial aspect of muscle development. In the absence of sufficient rest, the muscles may not fully recuperate, leading to a decrease in performance during the next set. In such cases, the muscles might tire prematurely, resulting in only less repetitions before reaching failure. This inadequate recovery period can limit the potential gains from the workout, hindering the overall muscle development process.

On the other hand, too much rest can also be detrimental to muscle activation. Prolonged rest periods may cause the muscles to cool down excessively, reducing their readiness for the next set. As a result, the muscles might not be fully engaged, leading to suboptimal performance and hindering the effectiveness of the exercise.

This is why finding the right balance in rest intervals is essential in a lifting session. The appropriate rest period allows the muscles to recover sufficiently while maintaining activation. This balance varies depending on factors like exercise intensity, training goals, and individual fitness levels. By identifying and adhering to the optimal rest periods, you enhance the effectiveness of your workouts and promote steady progress in muscle development over time.

The amount of rest you need depends on your specific goal, either muscular endurance, hypertrophy, or strength. Muscular endurance exercises demand shorter rest periods, benefiting those aiming to improve their capacity for sustained repetitions over an extended duration. Examples include high-intensity interval training exercises like burpees and sprints. Optimal rest periods for enhancing muscular endurance fall between 20 seconds and two minutes [4].

For those focused on muscular hypertrophy, which involves increasing muscle size, a slightly longer rest period is recommended. To induce muscular hypertrophy, rest periods of thirty to ninety seconds between sets are ideal [4].

Conversely, those seeking to boost muscular strength require even lengthier rest periods. In muscular strength training, the size of the muscle is not the focus, like it is in hypertrophy. Rather, the focus of muscular strength training is on increasing the amount of force produced. Strength is commonly measured by an individual's "one rep max," commonly abbreviated as 1RM, which is the maximum amount of weight that can be lifted for a single repetition. Longer rest periods enable athletes to sustain high levels of force production throughout each set. Typical rest periods for peak strength training performance lie within two to five minutes [4].

Once you identify your goal, whether it's muscular endurance, size, or strength, you can then tailor your training regimen to incorporate the appropriate rest periods. In doing so, you will optimize your performance and be able to give it your all for each set.

STRETCHING

Surprisingly, stretching is a highly controversial topic. Because of this, it becomes challenging to discern the truth and make informed decisions.

However, it is well known that stretching holds immense importance in maintaining muscle flexibility, strength, and overall health. It plays a pivotal role in enhancing joint range of motion, allowing your muscles to fully extend when you lift weights. Without adequate flexibility, relying on tight muscles to generate force increases the risk of muscular strains, tightness, damage, and pain.

In order to achieve proper range of motion and flexibility, you must stretch regularly. According to David Nolan, physical therapist at Massachusetts General Hospital, a program of three or four times each week is sufficient to improve flexibility. Because of society's sedentary lifestyle, the areas that get tight most often are the lower body muscles, like calves, hamstrings, hip flexors, and quads. Thus, these areas should be where you pay most of your attention. Additionally, stretching the shoulders, neck, and lower back regularly will avoid discomfort and injury.

A common misconception about stretching is that it can be achieved quickly. Because it takes several months for muscles to get tight, it will take several months for them to get flexible. Adopt a long-term perspective by incorporating stretching into your daily routine. Maybe start your day with a 10-minute session, or wind down before bed with some gentle yoga.

Understanding the optimal timing to stretch is another important factor. For years, the belief persisted that stretching before a workout was advantageous, aiding in muscle warm-up and preparation for physical activity. However, recent research has unveiled a contrasting truth, dependent on the type of stretching employed.

There are two primary types of stretching: static and dynamic. Static stretching involves holding a stretch without movement, while dynamic stretching entails actively moving muscles and joints through their full range of motion. While these two types of stretching are both beneficial, they serve different purposes.

Contrary to popular belief, doing static stretching as a warm-up before a workout has been shown to decrease athletic performance, as it impairs the body's ability to react swiftly [12]. One of the primary reasons for this is because when you hold a stretch for an extended period, the muscles are relaxed and elongated, which reduces their ability to contract forcefully. As a result, this temporary decrease in muscle strength can compromise the explosiveness and speed required for many exercises.

Additionally, static stretching can affect the body's neuromuscular system. During a workout or any physical activity, the body relies on quick and coordinated movements. However, when you perform static stretches before a workout, it creates a neuromuscular disconnect. This means that the communication between the muscles and the nervous system becomes momentarily disrupted, leading to a decrease in reaction time and coordination. Consequently, this can negatively impact performance in activities that require agility, quick reflexes, and swift reactions.

Research suggests that static stretching is better used after a workout, when muscles are already warm and pliable [12]. This is because the increased blood flow to the muscles enhances their adaptability to stretching. An analogy that illustrates this concept is bread dough, which is easier to mold and shape when warm and soft. Similarly, warmed muscles are more receptive to static stretches and are less likely to experience tightness and soreness. Therefore, incorporating post-workout static stretches will provide long-lasting relief from muscle soreness and tightness.

A more effective warm-up routine involves dynamic stretches, or movement-based stretches, which improve speed, reaction time, agility, and acceleration [12]. This is because dynamic stretching encompasses the active contraction of muscles and movement of joints through their complete range. The selection of dynamic stretches should align with the specific activity you plan to do, such as box jumps for basketball or volleyball, or leg swings for running.

Through embracing dynamic stretches as a warm-up and incorporating static stretches after a workout, you build the framework for optimizing athletic performance and maintaining muscular health.

FORM BEFORE WEIGHT

While it can be tempting to focus solely on the numbers and strive for lifting impressive weight, neglecting proper form will lead to detrimental consequences.

A telltale sign that form is being compromised during a lift is the use of momentum and swinging movements. When I see others resort to these techniques, it is a clear indication that the weight being lifted is too heavy.

While lifting impressively heavy weights may yield temporary satisfaction, using improper form not only diminishes the effectiveness of the exercise, but also increases the risk of injury. It shifts the focus away from the targeted muscles and places unnecessary strain on joints, tendons, and ligaments. Moreover, relying on momentum prevents the muscles from experiencing the full range of motion and reduces the time under tension, limiting the potential for muscle growth and strength development.

By executing movements with correct form, the intended muscle groups bear the appropriate load. This minimizes the risk of injury to other parts of the body and maximizes the effectiveness of the exercise. When someone demonstrates exceptional form while lifting lighter weights, it showcases a deep understanding of proper technique, body mechanics, and muscle engagement. Thus, from an observational standpoint, watching someone lift lighter weights with perfect form is exceedingly more impressive than lifting heavy weights with improper form.

Another important aspect of proper form is tempo, which involves controlling the timing for both the eccentric (lowering) and concentric (lifting) phases of an exercise. For instance, in the case of a bicep curl, a common tempo might involve lowering the weight for a duration of four seconds and then lifting it back up in one second.

By manipulating the tempo in this way, you introduce a new stimulus to your muscles. Slowing down the eccentric phase of an exercise increases the time under tension, intensifying the muscle fiber recruitment and muscle development. Conversely, accelerating the concentric phase can help generate power and explosiveness, emphasizing the strength aspect of the exercise. In this way, deliberate manipulation of the tempo of an exercise can be tailored to achieve specific fitness goals.

By incorporating various tempos within your training regimen, you add versatility and diversity to your workouts, enabling you to challenge your muscles from different angles. This promotes balanced muscular development and helps to prevent plateaus.

Furthermore, tempo manipulation can enhance the mind-muscle connection, as it causes you to become more conscious of how your muscles are engaging throughout each repetition. This increased focus not only improves the effectiveness of the exercise, but also promotes muscle symmetry and balance.

By prioritizing proper form, individuals can develop a strong mind-muscle connection, enhance body awareness, and cultivate a sustainable approach to fitness that prioritizes safety and effectiveness.

Equipped with this essential groundwork, you are now ready to practice, beginning with the six fundamental exercises. These exercises form the bedrock of any well-rounded fitness routine and offer a comprehensive approach to developing strength, stability, and overall functional fitness. They serve as a great starting point in creating a new workout routine that you can modify over time as you slowly target specific muscle groups to achieve specific tailored results.

THE PUSH-UP

I began my fitness journey not even being able to do a single push-up. That makes this exercise especially near and dear to my heart, as it was my first significant accomplishment in strength training.

The push-up engages the entire body, making it the king of bodyweight exercises. They are a fantastic exercise for developing upper body strength, as they primarily target the muscles of the chest, shoulders, and triceps. By regularly incorporating push-ups into your fitness routine, you can significantly increase the strength and endurance of these muscle groups.

Additionally, push-ups engage the core muscles, including the abdominals and lower back. As you maintain a straight body position, your core muscles are activated to stabilize your spine. This not only strengthens your core, but also improves overall stability and posture, reducing your risk of injuries.

The amazing part about this exercise is that it can be tailored to any strength level. Whether you are a beginner starting with modified pushups on your knees or an advanced athlete incorporating variations like diamond push-ups or one-arm push-ups, this movement can be tailored to challenge and progress your strength and skill.

A convenient aspect about push-ups is that they require no equipment. This means that they can be done anywhere, making them an excellent choice for those with limited access to a gym or exercise equipment. In fact, I rely on push-ups for workouts when I'm on vacation or when I don't have access to a gym.

Push-ups must be incorporated into your routine because they are a functionally beneficial exercise. In other words, they mimic movements commonly encountered in everyday life, such as pushing open a heavy door. For optimal health and strength, it's recommended that everyone should be able to do—or be working towards—at least 10 push-ups in a row.

HOW TO PERFORM

Start by positioning yourself on the floor with your hands slightly wider than shoulder-width apart, directly under your shoulders. Extend your legs straight behind you, resting on the balls of your feet. Brace your core by drawing your belly button towards your spine, ensuring your body forms a straight line from head to heels.

Lower your body towards the floor by bending your elbows. Keep your elbows close to your sides as you descend, focusing on controlling the movement. Continue lowering until your chest is just above the ground or as low as you can comfortably go.

Once you've reached the bottom position, push through your palms to you push your body back up. Keep your core engaged and maintain the straight line from head to heels. Fully extend your arms at the top of the movement without locking out your elbows.

Throughout the exercise, it's important to maintain proper form and technique. Avoid overarching or sagging your back, and keep your neck in a neutral, straightened position, looking at the ground. Focus on using your chest, shoulders, and triceps to generate the pushing movement. Remember to breathe naturally throughout the exercise, inhaling as you lower yourself down and exhaling as you push back up.

If you cannot yet do a push-up from your toes, modify the exercise by performing it on your knees instead. You can also practice the push-up by placing your hands on an elevated surface such as a bench or staircase. These variations still target the same muscle groups and allow you to gradually build strength.

Another way to improve strength for push-ups is to do isometric holds, which are static, non-moving pauses at the bottom of the push-up. Aim for an isometric hold of 10 seconds, gradually increasing time over the weeks. Regular practice and progressive overload will help you improve your push-up technique and increase strength.

THE PULL-UP

The pull-up is an incredibly important exercise for overall upper body strength and functional fitness. It primarily targets the muscles in the back, shoulders, and arms, including the latissimus dorsi, rhomboids, and biceps. Pull-ups not only help develop a strong and defined back, but they also improve posture, grip strength, and core stability.

While pull-ups can indeed be intimidating and seemingly impossible for beginners, it's essential to emphasize that with the right mindset, focused approach, and consistent training, anyone can master this challenging exercise.

Imagery is a powerful tool that cultivates the self-confidence and determined mindset necessary for making progress towards your first pull up. Close your eyes and imagine that you are standing underneath the pull-up bar. You reach up and wrap your hands around the metal bar until you have a firm grip. You lift your body into the air and feel your back muscles contracting and your chest rising. Your chin reaches the top of the bar. You slowly lower yourself down, feeling your exhausted muscles relaxing, and celebrate the satisfying achievement of conquering the pull-up.

The only way to get better at pull-ups is to simply do pull-ups. It's common for people to overlook this fact and instead concentrate solely on strengthening their back muscles through alternative exercises such as lat pull downs or cable rows. While these exercises can provide some assistance in making pull-ups more manageable, genuine progress and muscle memory is cultivated by actively practicing the specific movement you aim to improve.

By regularly practicing pull-ups, you train your body to adapt and become stronger in performing the exercise, leading to significant improvements in your pull-up performance over time.

HOW TO PERFORM

To perform a pull-up, start by finding a sturdy overhead bar. This can be a pull-up bar at the gym, a monkey bar at a playground, or a home pull-up bar.

Stand underneath the bar and reach up to grip it with an overhand grip, which is when your palms face away from you. Your hands should be slightly wider than shoulder-width apart, but you can also use an underhand grip if you prefer, which is called a chin-up.

Once you have a secure grip on the bar, jump up or use a step to get your chin above the bar and hang from it. Your arms should be fully extended, and your feet should be off the ground. This is your starting position.

To begin the pull-up, pull your body up towards the bar and drive your elbows down and back. Focus on using your back muscles, particularly your lats, to initiate the movement. As you pull yourself up, aim to bring your chin above the bar or as close to it as possible.

Once you've reached the top position, slowly lower yourself back down with control, fully extending your arms again. This completes one repetition of a pull-up.

Remember to maintain proper form throughout the exercise and avoid swinging or using momentum. Consistent practice and progressive overload will help you improve your strength and you will eventually be able to perform full pull-ups with ease.

However, for many beginners, pull-ups can be particularly challenging— trust me, I know. If you're unable to perform a pull-up, you can start with variations.

The most effective way to make progress towards completing your first pull up is by using the assistance machine. These machines typically have a platform for you to kneel or stand on, allowing you to control the amount of assistance for your pull-ups. Gradually decreasing the amount of assistance will allow you to build up towards eventually not requiring any at all.

If you don't have access to this type of machine, the next best solution is to use a resistance band. These are typically sold in a pack of several different levels of resistance that vary in thickness. The thicker the band, the more assistance it will provide for your pull-up.

When using the bands, first make sure that they are long enough to stretch out the full length of your body. Loop the band around the pull-up bar and secure it tightly. Step your foot in the bottom of the band and grab the pull-up bar with your hands. The band will provide enough assistance to allow you to complete a pull-up with perfect form. As you get stronger, you won't need as much assistance and can progress to the next thinnest band.

Using these variations will allow you to gradually work on building strength and progress towards unassisted pull-ups over time.

THE BENCH PRESS

The bench press is an essential exercise that holds significant importance in strength training and overall fitness. It primarily targets the muscles of the chest, shoulders, and triceps, while also engaging the core and upper back muscles as stabilizers.

By performing the bench press regularly and with proper form, you can develop upper body strength, power, and muscular endurance. This compound movement not only improves physical performance in various sports and activities but also promotes functional movement patterns in daily life. Moreover, the bench press is a highly versatile exercise, allowing for progressive overload and the ability to target different muscle groups through variations in grip width and bench angle.

Whether the goal is to build muscle, increase strength, or improve overall fitness, the bench press remains a cornerstone exercise that deserves a prominent place in any well-rounded training program.

HOW TO PERFORM

To perform a bench press with dumbbells, begin by sitting on a flat bench holding a dumbbell in each hand. The dumbbells should be resting on your knees.

Position your feet firmly on the ground, about shoulder-width apart. Take a deep breath in, and then breathe out as you lean back, bend your elbows, and push the dumbbells up to the sky. Your hands should be directly over your chest muscles, palms facing forward, and your elbows slightly bent. This starting position ensures stability and proper alignment.

Arch your lower back and dig your shoulder blades into the bench, in order to shift the weight to your chest muscles. This bracing action helps maintain a solid foundation throughout the exercise.

Now, inhale as you bring the dumbbells close to your sides. Control the tempo of the descent and make sure your arms are at a 45° angle from your body. Bring the dumbbells low enough to feel a stretch in your chest muscles, typically when the elbows are slightly below your shoulders. Your wrists should always be over your elbows.

At the bottom of the movement, drive through your chest muscles to push the dumbbells above your body. Maintain control and a smooth, fluid motion as you press the dumbbells upward.

As you reach the top of the movement, the dumbbells should be about an inch apart. Pause briefly to feel the contraction in your chest muscles. Focus on squeezing your chest to fully engage the targeted muscles. Avoid locking out your elbows at the top; instead, keep a slight bend in your elbows to maintain tension in your chest muscles and prevent strain on the joints.

Remember to select a weight that challenges you, but still allows you to maintain proper form. Gradually increase the weight as you become stronger and more comfortable with the exercise. Consistency and gradual progression will help you improve your strength and technique in the bench press with dumbbells.

By following these steps and focusing on proper form, you can effectively target your chest muscles, improve upper body strength, and maximize the benefits of the bench press with dumbbells.

THE OVERHEAD PRESS

The overhead press, also known as the shoulder press, holds great significance in strength training and overall fitness. It primarily targets the deltoid muscles of the shoulders, along with the triceps and upper back. This compound movement also engages the core muscles as stabilizers, enhancing overall body stability and balance.

Additionally, the overhead press promotes functional strength. By practicing this exercise and gradually increasing strength over time, we also improve everyday movements such as reaching for items on high shelves or raising a child onto your shoulders. Thus, this exercise lays the groundwork for injury prevention and reduces the likelihood of strains or overuse injuries in the future.

Executing this exercise with proper technique, focus, and progressive overload is not only an investment in present gains, but also an investment in our future well-being and functionality.

HOW TO PERFORM

To perform an overhead press, start by sitting on a sturdy bench or chair with your feet planted firmly on the ground. Keep your spine straight and brace your core. Take a dumbbell in each hand and rest them on your thighs, bell pointing up.

Next, quickly raise your knees to provide the initial momentum to get the dumbbells above your head. Breathe out to help get the weights up.

Make sure your palms are facing forward, and your elbows are slightly bent. It's important to avoid locking out your elbows at this point to prevent unnecessary strain. This starting position allows you to have proper control and stability.

Lower the dumbbells slowly back to the starting position while inhaling deeply. You are at the bottom of the movement when your elbows are just beneath shoulder-height. Your wrists should always be over your elbows.

Remember to choose a weight that challenges you, but still allows you to maintain proper form. If you're a beginner, it's a good idea to start with lighter weights and gradually increase the resistance as you become more comfortable and stronger.

By following these steps and focusing on proper form, you can effectively target your shoulder muscles, improve upper body strength, and maximize the benefits of the overhead press with dumbbells. Remember to listen to your body, start with a weight you can handle safely, and progress gradually over time.

THE SQUAT

The squat is one of the most crucial and indispensable movements in strength training and overall fitness. It primarily targets the muscles of the lower body, including the quadriceps, hamstrings, and glutes, while also engaging the core and back muscles as stabilizers.

By incorporating squats into a workout routine, you can develop lower body strength, power, and muscular endurance. This compound movement not only improves athletic performance in activities like running, jumping, and lifting, but also enhances everyday functional movements such as sitting down, standing up, and bending. The squat exercise also promotes proper alignment and balance, leading to improved posture and reduced risk of injuries.

Executing correct form during a squat depends on your individual body and the unique way it moves. Many people will claim that there is only one perfect way to do a squat, but they are wrong. Similar to the inherited traits of facial structure and hair color, body stature is genetically passed down from parents. For instance, people with longer femurs, which are the bones in the upper legs, may find it necessary to incorporate a more pronounced forward lean during their squat technique. Nevertheless, there are certain guidelines that are universally applicable, regardless of one's body type.

HOW TO PERFORM

To perform a squat, start by standing with your feet shoulder-width apart or slightly wider. If needed, position your toes pointing slightly outward to accommodate your natural range of motion.

Engage your core muscles by bracing your core. If you don't know how to do this, pretend someone is about to punch you. This will cause you to immediately contract your stomach muscles and brace for impact. Use this tension throughout your squat in order to maximize your strength and power output.

Initiate the squat from your hips and bend your knees. Lower your body by pushing your hips back and down, as if you're sitting back into an imaginary chair. Keep your weight balanced evenly on both feet and ensure that your knees are tracking in line with your toes.

As you descend, aim to lower your hips until your thighs are parallel to the ground, or as close to parallel as your mobility allows. It's important to maintain control and stability throughout the movement, avoiding any sudden or jerky motions.

During the squat, keep your chest lifted and your gaze forward to maintain proper spinal alignment. Avoid rounding your back or excessively leaning forward, as this can place unnecessary strain on your lower back.

Once you've reached the bottom position of the squat, exhale and push through your heels to drive yourself back up to the starting position. Focus on engaging your leg muscles, particularly your quadriceps and glutes, to initiate the ascent. Maintain a controlled pace and avoid locking your knees at the top of the movement.

In order to improve your squat form, practice squatting in front of a mirror. Analyze from different angles, paying careful attention to your form and bar path. You can also record yourself or have someone take a video of you with your phone camera to provide a different perspective.

When performing squats, it's important to start with a weight that you can handle safely. If you're new to squats, bodyweight can be a great starting point to develop proper form and technique. As you become more comfortable and confident, you can progress to using additional weight, such as a barbell or dumbbells, to further challenge your muscles. Consistency and progressive overload will help you build strength and improve your squat technique over time.

THE DEADLIFT

The deadlift is called the "deadlift" because you are quite literally picking up dead weight from the ground. It is an exercise of paramount importance in strength training and overall fitness because it targets many muscles, including the hamstrings, glutes, and lower back, as well as the core and grip strength.

This compound movement also enhances everyday functionality, improving strength and stability in tasks like picking up a small child from the floor or putting a case of water on the bottom shelf of your shopping cart. Deadlifting also promotes optimal posture and spinal alignment, as it requires the engagement of the core and back muscles for stability.

Trap bar deadlifts and straight bar deadlifts differ in grip and body positioning. Trap bar deadlifts, as shown in the picture, typically allow for a more neutral wrist and grip position, which reduces strain on the lower back and provides a more comfortable lifting experience. Straight bar deadlifts require a traditional overhand or mixed grip, which may put more emphasis on the lower back and hamstrings, but also demand proper form and lower back strength.

By incorporating deadlifts into your workout routine, you will develop exceptional full-body strength, power, and muscular endurance.

HOW TO PERFORM

Begin by standing in front of the barbell with your feet about hip-width apart. Squat down by bending at the knees to grip the barbell slightly wider than shoulder-width.

Engage your core and activate your back muscles by attempting to break the barbell in half. This cue will rotate your shoulder blades back and activate your latissimus dorsi, which prevents your lower back from rounding and straining. Another cue that might help avoid this common cause of pain is to pretend like you are squeezing an orange in your armpits during the setup and execution of the lift.

Push the floor away with your feet as you pull the weight up. Keep your chest up and shoulder blades retracted. Avoid locking the knees on the ascent by keeping a slight bend in them when fully extended.

On the descent, push your butt back as far as it will go, keeping a slight bend in your knees. Let the barbell maintain close contact with your lower body, scraping your shins and thighs, and lower it to the ground. Do a light tap on the ground and repeat.

Maintaining proper alignment and positioning of the barbell in relation to your center of gravity is crucial throughout the entirety of the movement. The barbell should ideally be positioned directly over the midline of your foot, ensuring that your center of gravity remains balanced and stable. Deviating from this alignment by holding the weight too far away from your center of gravity can lead to an increased strain on your lower back, potentially resulting in discomfort or injury.

This principle of keeping the weight centered applies not only to deadlifts but to every exercise you perform. By adhering to this fundamental rule, you promote optimal biomechanics, minimize unnecessary stress on your body, and create a solid foundation for safe and effective movement. Remember, maintaining proper alignment and positioning is an essential aspect of maximizing the benefits and minimizing the risks associated with any exercise routine.

NICKI BRIGHT

08
WORKOUT PROGRAMS

Imagine walking into the gym without a clue about what to do. You might end up wandering aimlessly, wasting time, and feeling unsure about which exercises are best for your goals. This lack of structure can lead to frustration and ultimately hinder your fitness journey.

To prevent this, it's crucial to come prepared with a well-designed workout plan. By having a plan in place, you can optimize your time at the gym and ensure that every minute spent exercising counts toward your goals.

When it comes to planning a workout, simplicity is key. Even for advanced programs, always start with one or two fundamental exercises. Compound exercises are well known for their high metabolic and physical demands, so by starting your workout with one or two of these movements, you can take advantage of your peak energy and strength levels. This allows you to give your best effort and achieve optimal results.

Next in your workout should be variation exercises. These exercises maintain the focus on engaging multiple muscle groups, with some modifications or variations to target specific areas or enhance the challenge.

Finally, incorporating isolation exercises can further isolate specific muscle groups, providing a more targeted and intense workout. These exercises allow for precise targeting of individual muscles, enabling you to work on muscle imbalances or specific areas of weakness. By including both compound variations and isolation exercises in your routine after the initial compound exercises, you can ensure a well-rounded training session.

Keep in mind that this book only provides guidance on form and technique for the six fundamental exercises. The fundamentals provide the basic building blocks for a foundation of strength and are included in each workout (bolded). On this note, you might not recognize some of the variation and isolation exercises listed in the following programs. If that's the case, you'll have to wait for my next book. In the meantime, be proactive by watching videos or reading articles for each of the exercises that are unfamiliar to you.

Now that you have a comprehensive understanding of the six fundamental exercises and an understanding of how to structure a workout, you are ready to create a training program. To get you started on the right track, I have provided three generic programs tailored to experience levels. By following these programs, you will be able to establish a consistent routine and develop the habit of regular exercise.

BEGINNER

This weekly workout plan is specifically designed for people who are new to weightlifting or have less than one month of experience in the gym.

DAY 1	DAY 2	DAY 3	DAY 4	DAY 5	DAY 6	DAY 7
Full Body	Rest	Rest	Full Body	Rest	Full Body	Rest

FULL BODY WORKOUT

A: Upper body fundamental exercise *(dumbbell bench press)*
B: Lower body fundamental exercise *(squat with barbell)*
C1: Accessory lower body exercise *(single leg split squat with the front foot elevated on 5" box)*
C2: Accessory upper body exercise *(dumbbell bicep curl with barbell)*
D1: Accessory lower body exercise *(leg press on machine)*
D2: Accessory upper body exercise *(tricep extension with cable and straight bar)*

Full-body workouts hold great importance for beginners when initiating their weightlifting journey. These types of workouts involve engaging multiple muscle groups and performing exercises that target various areas of the body within a single session. Additionally, full-body workouts allow beginners to learn and practice a wide range of exercises that target different muscle groups.

When you see an exercise labeled with a letter and a number, it signifies a superset. For example, in the above workout, C1 represents the first exercise, while C2 is the subsequent exercise to be performed right after, without any rest in between.

If you don't know how much weight to start with or how many reps to do, begin with three sets of 12 reps for each exercise. In other words, choose a weight that allows you to *only* get a maximum of 12 reps. If you can do more than 12 reps with the selected weight while maintaining proper form, increase the weight until you can't do the 13th rep.

In this program, you will notice a significant focus on unilateral movements, which means using only one arm or leg. This emphasis stems from the recognition that beginners often experience muscular imbalances. For instance, if you have a dominant right side, you may be accustomed to activities such as writing, catching, and throwing predominantly with your right hand. Over time, this can lead to a notable disparity in strength between your right and left arms.

Consequently, it becomes crucial to address and rectify these imbalances early on, as they have the potential to contribute to injuries when lifting progressively heavier weights. By incorporating unilateral exercises, you can effectively target and correct these discrepancies, promoting improved overall strength and reducing the risk of future harm.

Weightlifting can be exhilarating and motivating, but it is crucial to listen to your body's signals and honor when your body needs rest. Beginners commonly get caught up in the misconception that going to the gym every single day is necessary to achieve results. Starting with a minimum of two to three strength training sessions per week is an excellent foundation.

Resting on your off days allows your muscles to repair and rebuild, reducing the risk of injury and improving overall performance in the long run. This gentle approach also allows you to gradually adapt to the gym environment, establish a manageable schedule that suits your lifestyle, and build confidence in handling weights.

By starting with two sessions each week, you also minimize the risk of burning out quickly and abandoning your new workout routine after just a couple of weeks. Consistency and sustainability are key factors in long-term success, so it's essential to find a pace that works for you and sets you up for continued progress.

The rest days in this program are purposefully scheduled to create the ideal balance of work and rest, giving you one to two days between workouts to recover. On your rest days, only do physical activities that promote relaxation, such as gentle stretching, leisurely walks, or mindfulness practices. This deliberate rest not only aids in physical recovery, but also nurtures mental well-being and fosters renewed motivation for future workouts.

INTERMEDIATE

The program outlined here is specifically tailored for people who have been weightlifting for about six months to several years.

DAY 1	DAY 2	DAY 3	DAY 4	DAY 5	DAY 6	DAY 7
Upper Body	Active Rest	Full Body	Rest	Lower Body	Active Rest	Rest

UPPER BODY WORKOUT

A: Fundamental exercise *(pull-up)*
B: Fundamental exercise *(dumbbell bench press)*
C: Accessory exercise *(seated row on machine)*
D1: Accessory exercise *(lateral raise with dumbbells)*
D2: Accessory exercise *(rear delt row on machine)*

LOWER BODY WORKOUT

A: Fundamental exercise *(squat)*
B: Fundamental exercise *(deadlift)*
D: Accessory exercise *(heel-elevated step-up)*
E1: Accessory exercise *(quad extension on machine)*
E2: Accessory exercise *(hamstring curl on machine)*

FULL BODY WORKOUT

A: Upper body fundamental exercise *(dumbbell bench press)*
B: Lower body fundamental exercise *(squat with barbell)*
C1: Accessory lower body exercise *(single leg split squat with the front foot elevated on 5" box)*
C2: Accessory upper body exercise *(dumbbell bicep curl with barbell)*
D1: Accessory lower body exercise *(leg press on machine)*
D2: Accessory upper body exercise *(tricep extension with cable and straight bar)*

This program incorporates a strategic split between upper body and lower body workouts, complemented by a full-body workout. The intention behind this division is to focus on more specific muscle groups during each session.

When performing an upper body-only workout, the blood flow intensifies towards the upper extremities to support the exerted force and work being generated. This increased blood circulation aids in supplying the necessary nutrients and oxygen to the targeted muscles. The goal is to maximize the duration during which the body remains in this depleted state.

This level of fatigue is particularly relevant for hypertrophy, the process of muscle growth. By subjecting the muscles to intense exertion and depleting their energy stores, the body signals the need for adaptation and repair. This triggers the cellular mechanisms that stimulate muscle growth and the synthesis of new muscle tissue. Thus, by focusing on one portion of the body at a time and creating an environment of fatigue and depletion, this program optimizes the conditions necessary for hypertrophy and muscle development.

The rest days in this program are strategically sandwiched between workout days, allowing yourself a day or two to relax and recover. This program also introduces the concept of "active rest" days, which offer a refreshing change of pace. On these days, instead of remaining completely sedentary, you should do alternative forms of exercise such as hiking, running, swimming, or cycling.

These activities not only provide a break from the specific movements of weightlifting, but also challenge your muscles in new and exciting ways. Doing different activities on your active rest days helps prevent monotony and mental fatigue, allowing you to stay motivated and enthusiastic about your fitness journey. It also stimulates different muscle groups, promoting overall strength and conditioning.

Remember, the key is to strike a balance between rest and active recovery. While active rest days offer an opportunity for different forms of exercise, it is crucial to listen to your body and avoid pushing yourself to the point of exhaustion. Allow these days to be a pleasurable break from your regular routine while still providing the necessary rest and recovery your body needs.

ADVANCED

This program is specifically designed for those who have been lifting weights for a year or more and are experienced at lifting weights.

DAY 1	DAY 2	DAY 3	DAY 4	DAY 5	DAY 6	DAY 7
Push	Pull	Legs	Rest	Push	Pull	Rest

PUSH

A: Fundamental exercise *(dumbbell chest press)*
B: Fundamental exercise *(overhead press with dumbells)*
C: Accessory exercise *(dumbbell lateral raise)*
D: Accessory exercise *(seated chest press on machine)*
E: Accessory exercise *(tricep extension with cable and straight bar)*

PULL

A: Fundamental exercise *(pull-up)*
B: Fundamental exercise *(deadlift)*
C: Accessory exercise *(cable back row with close grip)*

D: Accessory exercise *(seated low row on machine)*
E: Accessory exercise *(dumbbell rear delt flyes)*

LEGS

A: Fundamental exercise *(squat)*
B: Fundamental exercise *(deadlift)*
C: Accessory exercise *(hip thrust with barbell)*
D: Accessory exercise *(romanian deadlift with dumbellst)*
E: Accessory exercise *(quad extension on machine)*

The push, pull, legs (PPL) split is one of the most common workout splits due to its effectiveness in balancing muscle groups and providing adequate recovery. This split divides workouts into three main categories: push exercises, pull exercises, and leg exercises.

The "push" workout focuses on exercises that primarily involve pushing movements, such as chest presses, overhead presses, and triceps exercises. These exercises target muscles like the chest, shoulders, and triceps.

The "pull" workout, on the other hand, emphasizes exercises that involve pulling movements, including exercises for the back, biceps, and rear deltoids. Examples include pull-ups, rows, and bicep curls.

Lastly, the "legs" workout concentrates on lower body exercises, such as squats, lunges, deadlifts, and calf raises. This targets the muscles in the legs, including the quadriceps, hamstrings, glutes, and calves.

The PPL split allows for effective distribution of workload and recovery. By dividing exercises into different categories, it helps ensure that each muscle group receives adequate rest while you focus on training other areas. This can aid in muscle growth and strength development.

Furthermore, this split provides a level of versatility, as it allows individuals to customize their workouts based on their specific goals and preferences. For instance, you can train each muscle group twice a week, resulting in more rapid progress. On the other hand, a three-day-per-week routine allows for a slower-paced approach, providing more recovery time and flexibility in scheduling workouts.

While you may expect an advanced program to have a workout scheduled every day, it's important to recognize that exceeding five strength training sessions per week is not necessarily optimal for achieving maximum hypertrophy or strength. While it's true that some elite athletes or bodybuilding competitors follow rigorous workout routines that include six to seven sessions per week—and occasionally even double workouts in a single day—there is a specific context in which these routines are required.

Intense and high-frequency training routines are typically implemented for a relatively short duration and with a specific goal in mind, such as preparing for a competition or achieving peak physical performance for a specific event. The individual's advanced training status, recovery capacity, and close supervision from expert coaches are also taken into account.

For most people, especially those who are not professional athletes or bodybuilding competitors, you must consider factors such as your fitness level, recovery ability, and if you have any lifestyle constraints. Nevertheless, a personalized workout program and clear plan are all you need to make progress in the gym.

Rest is of utmost importance in the advanced program as it allows your body to recover and adapt following intense workouts. During these strength training sessions, your muscles experience microtears and metabolic stress. It's during time that you rest that these muscles repair and rebuild, leading to growth and increased strength.

Without sufficient rest, your body may not have enough time to adequately recover. This increases your risk of overtraining, fatigue, and potential injuries. By incorporating two to three dedicated rest days cushioned between workouts, you provide ample time for your body to repair and rejuvenate, just in time for the next workout.

The rest days also serve as an opportunity for your central nervous system to recover. Intense workouts can put significant stress on your nervous system, affecting its ability to efficiently transmit signals to your muscles. By giving it enough rest, you allow your nervous system the chance to restore its function, ensuring optimal performance in subsequent workouts.

Furthermore, resting plays a significant role in preventing burnout and mental fatigue. Pushing yourself to the limit day after day without allowing for proper recovery can lead to decreased motivation, diminished performance, and even a higher likelihood of quitting. Incorporating dedicated rest days will help you maintain a healthy balance between physical exertion and rejuvenation, ensuring the sustainability and longevity of your fitness journey.

Keep in mind that rest days do not imply complete inactivity. While they are intended to provide a break from your workouts, they can still include light activities such as walking, swimming, gentle stretching, and light yoga. These low-impact exercises promote blood flow, aid in muscle recovery, and help alleviate any residual muscle soreness.

The most effective way to plan and track your workouts is by using a workout program template. This will provide a structured framework for organizing your exercises, sets, reps, and other important notes. Using templates will help you create a clear roadmap for your workouts and allow you to easily monitor your progress over time.

Use the following page to make copies and record your workouts.

FINDING FITNESS FREEDOM

Date:

Exercise	Set	Weight	Reps
	1		
	2		
	3		
	1		
	2		
	3		
	1		
	2		
	3		
	1		
	2		
	3		
	1		
	2		
	3		
	1		
	2		
	3		

Having a solid grasp of the six fundamental exercises and establishing a well-structured workout program provides a strong foundation for your fitness journey. However, to truly excel and make continuous strides in your performance, you must be able to apply more advanced training concepts.

PROGRESSIVE OVERLOAD

Training consistently is crucial for making strength progress, but simply training without implementing progressive overload will limit your potential for maximum results.

Progressive overload is a fundamental concept in strength training that involves gradually increasing the demands placed on muscles over time. When you lift weights, your muscles adapt to the stress by becoming stronger and more efficient. However, once your muscles have adapted to a certain level of stress, they require a new stimulus to continue growing and getting stronger. This is where progressive overload comes into play.

Progressive overload involves progressively increasing the intensity, volume, or complexity of your workouts to continually challenge your muscles. This can be achieved through various methods, such as increasing the weight you lift, performing more repetitions, adding additional sets, shortening rest periods, changing the tempo (speed), or incorporating more challenging exercises. By progressively increasing the intensity of workout through these methods, the muscles are continually stimulated and forced to adapt, leading to improvements in strength, size, and overall muscle development.

Without incorporating progressive overload, progress may slow down or plateau. This is because when the body becomes accustomed to a certain level of stress during workouts, it adapts to meet those demands, resulting in a reduced stimulus for growth. By progressively increasing the demand on your muscles, you'll be able to continue challenging your body, prompting it to continually adapt and make gains in strength and muscle size.

In order to effectively implement progressive overload into your workout routine, you must keep a record of each workout. Whether it's an app on your phone or a simple pen and paper, documentation is the only way to make sure that each session is building upon the previous one and that progressive overload is consistently implemented. By recording the exercises performed, the weights lifted, the number of repetitions and sets completed, and other relevant details, you can easily monitor your progress over time, allowing you to identify areas of improvement and make informed adjustments to your training programs.

FAILURE

Failure, in terms of weightlifting, refers to the inability to complete a specific exercise or lift with proper form and technique. It occurs when the lifter reaches a point—typically the last repetition, or rep—in which they can no longer perform the exercise out of fatigue or muscle exhaustion.

Despite the negative connotations associated with the word "failure," reaching a point of failure while performing your last repetition is not a bad thing. In fact, reaching the point of failure serves as a clear indication of a successful strength training session.

Reaching failure indicates that you have exerted maximum effort and reached the point where your muscles can no longer perform the movement with proper form and technique. Thus, failing a lift provides valuable feedback about your current strength levels, allowing you to assess your progress and identify areas for improvement. By recognizing where you fail, you can target those specific muscles or movements in your training routine and implement strategies to address any weaknesses or limitations.

When you consistently challenge your muscles by lifting weights that bring you to the brink of failure, you create a stimulus that signals your body to adapt and become stronger over time. This process, known as progressive overload, is crucial for making strength gains and building muscle mass.

Keep in mind that it's important to approach failure with caution and prioritize safety. It's recommended to have a spotter or use appropriate safety equipment, especially when performing heavy compound lifts like squats, bench presses, or deadlifts. Additionally, it's essential to maintain proper form and technique throughout your lifts to minimize the risk of injury.

TRAINING TOOLS

In the beginning of your fitness journey, you don't need much to make progress and see results. All you need is your body, some resistance, and a determined mindset. However, as you progressively handle heavier loads and your strength improves, you may encounter plateaus in progress. This is when knowing when to incorporate specific lifting tools, like lifting straps and weight belts, becomes important.

Lifting straps are straps made of fabric or leather that are looped around the wrist and then wrapped around a barbell or dumbbell handle. They are used to enhance grip strength and prevent the bar from slipping out of the hands, especially during exercises like deadlifts, rows, and pull-ups. This is because your legs and back are likely much stronger than your hands. Using lifting straps allows you to focus on the targeted muscles rather than struggling to maintain your hold.

To utilize lifting straps effectively, begin by preparing the lifting straps, ensuring they are untangled and creating a loop by passing one end through the loop or opening at the other end. Slip this loop over your wrist and position them securely, allowing the excess length to hang down.

Next, wrap the dangling end of the strap tightly around the bar or handle of the weight you will be lifting, ensuring a snug fit. Grip the bar or handle with your hands, placing your fingers around it, with the lifting straps positioned between your fingers and the bar.

With the straps properly secured, perform the exercise with proper form and technique and witness the power of the straps, enabling you to handle heavier weights effectively without your grip weakening.

Weight belts serve a different purpose, specifically when performing exercises that involve loads surpassing your bodyweight. These belts play a critical role in supporting your lower back and core during these movements.

By providing external stability and compression, weight belts help maintain proper posture and spinal alignment, reducing the risk of injury. They effectively distribute the load and minimize stress on the lower back, allowing you to lift heavy weights with increased safety and confidence.

To properly use a weight belt, begin by selecting a belt that fits snugly around your waist, with an adjustable buckle or closure. Position the weight belt around your waist, making sure it sits comfortably on your lower back and abdomen, positioned on the area just above your hip bones. Fasten the buckle or closure securely, ensuring the weight belt is firmly in place.

As you do the exercise, whether it's squats, deadlifts, or overhead presses, the weight belt will provide additional support and stability to your core and lower back. It helps maintain proper posture, alignment, and spinal integrity, reducing the risk of injury. Remember to breathe properly during the exercise, allowing your diaphragm to expand and contract freely. When the exercise is complete, unfasten the weight belt and remove it from your waist.

It's important to note that the use of lifting straps and weight belts should not be relied upon as a substitute for developing strength. These tools are meant to supplement your training when necessary, particularly for specific movements or heavier loads that require additional assistance. As your strength and proficiency improve, you should gradually reduce reliance on these tools and focus on developing natural grip strength and core stability.

THE BASICS OF NUTRITION

Every day is an opportunity for you to build your body and it all starts with what you feed it. Nutrition is so important, in fact, that the ability to control and regulate dietary habits is what differentiates those who achieve their goals and those who do not.

In my experience training both myself and clients, I've learned that the impact of intense workouts and rigorous training on the overall outcome is a mere 20%. Surprisingly, the remaining 80% comes down to nutrition. This means that it's not just about pushing your limits in the gym; it's about fueling your body with the right nutrients.

In the words of Ocean Robbins, "When you eat the standard American diet, you get the standard American diseases." Robbins, a prominent advocate for healthy and sustainable living and co-founder of the Food Revolution Network, urges us to recognize the undeniable truth behind this statement.

In a world filled with abundant dietary options, it can be easy to succumb to convenience, indulging in processed and unhealthy foods that have become all too commonplace in the standard American diet. However, these dietary choices come at a cost, leading to an abundance of health issues that have unfortunately become the norm.

To break free from this cycle, nutrition must be prioritized as a foundational pillar of fitness freedom. When you embrace a nourishing diet that aligns with your goals, you'll witness the power it holds in propelling you towards success. Neglecting proper nutrition can severely hinder progress, while prioritizing it can unlock your full potential.

Keep in mind that the purpose of this chapter is not to tell you explicitly what to eat. Instead, my goal is to provide you with knowledge derived from science-based research and broaden your understanding of nutrition. By grasping the fundamental importance of food, you will gain the confidence necessary to make informed decisions the next time you are navigating the aisles of the grocery store.

The World Health Organization states that the fundamental cause of obesity and being overweight is an energy imbalance between calories consumed and calories burned. In other words, if you eat more calories than you burn in a day, you're going to gain weight. If you eat less calories than you burn in a day, you're going to lose weight.

The amazing thing is, your body will burn a lot of calories every day, even if you were to lay on the couch and do nothing at all. Your body needs fuel in order to perform necessary metabolic functions, such as breathing, beating your heart, and supplying blood to your body. In fact, the largest contributor to your daily caloric burn comes from your basal metabolic rate, or BMR, at a surprising 70%.

The second largest contributor is physical activity, representing a measly 20%. This means that by prioritizing factors that affect your BMR, such as maintaining muscle mass, proper nutrition, and adequate sleep, you create a solid foundation for a healthy metabolism and sustainable weight management.

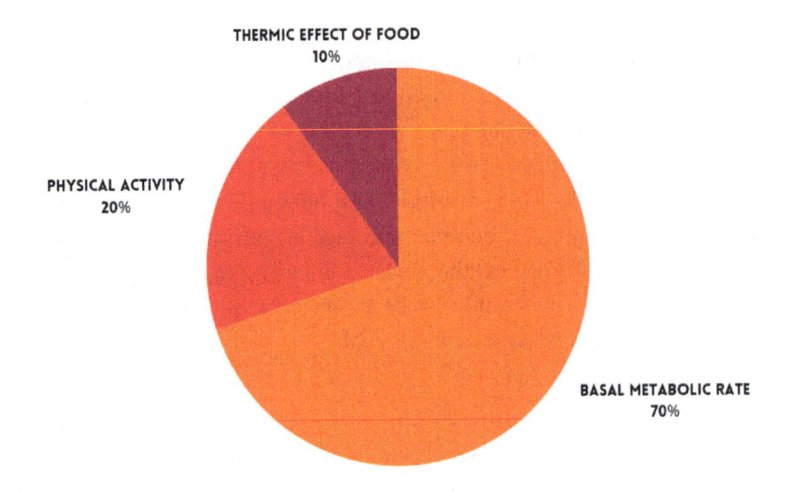

THERMIC EFFECT OF FOOD
10%

PHYSICAL ACTIVITY
20%

BASAL METABOLIC RATE
70%

This revelation is precisely why I strive to change the way my clients approach food. Instead of believing the notion that consuming a 200-calorie slice of pizza requires a grueling thirty-minute run to "burn it off," a healthier mindset is to understand that all calories consumed, whether nutritionally beneficial or not, contribute to your daily caloric intake.

Therefore, we must aim to strike a balance between calories consumed and calories burned, as *that* is the key to achieving any fitness goal. Understanding that the body is already expending calories even at rest allows us to cultivate a healthy relationship with food, making rigid compensatory exercise routines unnecessary.

The remaining 10% of your caloric expenditure is from the thermal effect of food, or TEF. This refers to the increase in energy expenditure that occurs during the process of digesting, absorbing, and metabolizing food. When we consume food, our bodies expend energy to break down complex nutrients into simpler forms, transport them, and convert them into usable energy or store them for later use. The thermic effect can vary depending on the macronutrient composition of the meal. Protein tends to have the highest thermal effect, followed by carbohydrates and then fats.

The TEF makes up such a minor portion of our daily caloric expenditure that it doesn't need to be factored into daily caloric needs. However, by understanding the TEF, we can better appreciate the energy cost associated with the digestion and metabolism of different nutrients.

To understand how many calories you need, begin by establishing your BMR. To do this, you can use an online calculator or manually with the Harris-Benedict formula.

MEN
66.47 + (6.24 × weight in pounds) + (12.7 × height in inches) − (6.75 × age in years)

WOMEN
65.51 + (4.35 × weight in pounds) + (4.7 × height in inches) − (4.7 × age in years)

Once you calculate BMR, you know how many calories you burn simply by existing. However, you do much more than just exist—most days at least. You might spend time gardening, cleaning the house, taking the stairs instead of the elevator, walking your kids to school, or cycling to work. Engaging in these activities contributes to your total daily caloric expenditure. Moreover, if you are an active individual who enjoys jogging, swimming, or attending fitness classes regularly, these workouts add an additional layer to your daily caloric burn. Thus, it becomes essential to consider daily movement as a significant contributor to your overall daily caloric expenditure.

You can use several online calculators to help you with this, but for reference, these are the values and formulas.

ACTIVITY LEVEL VALUES
Sedentary (0 workouts/week) = 1.3
Lightly Active (1-2 workouts/week) = 1.5
Active (3-4 workouts/week) = 1.7
Very Active (5-7 workouts/week) = 2.0

Daily Caloric Requirement = BMR x Activity Level Value

Your BMR is multiplied by your activity level value to provide your daily caloric requirement. This is the amount of calories you would need in a day in order to maintain your current physique.

However, if your goal to go beyond mere maintenance and take your physique to the next level, you can now adjust your caloric intake according to your specific goals. For those aiming to shed excess weight, a caloric deficit is key. This means reducing the number of calories consumed below the amount required to maintain. In doing so, the body is compelled to tap into stored fat for energy, leading to weight loss over time. This reduction in caloric intake can be achieved through a combination of dietary changes, portion control, and mindful eating.

Conversely, those seeking to increase their weight, whether to build muscle or add healthy mass, need to be in a caloric surplus. This entails consuming more calories than the body burns in a day, creating an excess of energy that can be used for muscle repair and growth. The additional calories should be sourced from nutrient-dense foods, such as lean proteins, healthy fats, and complex carbohydrates, to ensure the weight gain is achieved healthily.

Keep in mind that achieving your goals through the manipulation of caloric intake requires following a dedicated strength training routine. Neglecting to prioritize building lean muscle when consuming a surplus of calories may lead to the undesired outcome of accumulating excess fat. The body has a mechanism to store excess calories as energy, and without the breakdown and rebuilding of muscle fibers through strength training, these surplus calories will be directed towards fat storage rather than muscle growth.

Conversely, being in a calorie deficit without strength training can result in an unflattering condition known as "skinny fat." This occurs when there is a lack of adequate calories to support muscle development, resulting in a body composition that appears relatively lean, but lacks muscle definition and shape. Thus, by combining proper nutrition with strength training, you can effectively make progress towards achieving your fitness goals.

The rate of your progress is directly influenced by the number of calories you consume in either a surplus or a deficit. Fast progress requires an extreme approach, while gradual progress involves a moderate approach. You can use the following table to tailor your caloric intake towards achieving your goals at your desired rate.

Goal	Calorie surplus/deficit	Pounds gained/lost each week	Pounds gained/lost each month
Fast Weight Loss	-500	-1	-4
Slow Weight Loss	-300	-0.6	-2.4
Some Weight Loss	-200	-0.4	-1.6
No Weight Loss or Gain	0	0	0
Some Weight Gain	+200	0.4	1.6
Slow Weight Gain	+300	0.6	2.4
Fast Weight Gain	+500	1	4

Calories are made up of macronutrients, the fundamental building blocks of our diet. They can be categorized into three essential groups: proteins, carbohydrates, and fats. These macronutrients, or "macros," not only provide our bodies with vital nutrients, but also serve as a source of energy. However, each macronutrient differs in its caloric density, or the amount of energy it stores. Proteins and carbohydrates each have four calories per gram, while fats have nine calories per gram.

Understanding macronutrients in depth is crucial because a balanced intake of proteins, carbohydrates, and fats is essential for optimal health, performance, and body composition. By exploring the intricacies of these macronutrients and mastering the art of balancing them in our diet, we discover their powerful role in unlocking energy, optimizing performance, and shaping our bodies.

PROTEIN

When it comes to building muscle, finding the right balance of macronutrients in your diet is of utmost importance. However, it can be overwhelming to figure out the right combination of proteins, carbohydrates, and fats to support muscle growth effectively.

To simplify the approach, prioritize protein over all other macronutrients. Protein is the building block of muscle, and consuming enough of it is essential for muscle repair and growth. When you lift weights, your muscle fibers experience micro-tears. Protein provides the necessary amino acids to repair these tears, leading to muscle recovery and ultimately muscle hypertrophy (growth).

By making protein the central focus of your diet, you ensure that your body has a steady supply of essential amino acids to support muscle repair and growth after each workout. Include a variety of high-quality protein sources, such as lean meats, poultry, fish, eggs, dairy, and plant-based proteins like legumes and tofu.

If you're unsure about how much protein you need, a good starting point is consuming one gram of protein per pound of body weight. For instance, if you weigh 150 pounds, aim for around 150 grams of protein each day.

In addition to focusing on the absolute grams of protein, it's also important to consider the proportion of protein in relation to your total calorie intake. Protein should account for approximately 25% to 35% of your daily calories. For example, if your daily caloric needs amount to 2,000 calories, and you aim for 30% of those calories to come from protein, your protein intake should be approximately 150 grams (30% of 2,000 calories).

When it comes to protein, you may have heard about the concept of the "anabolic window." This concept, popular in the bodybuilding community, suggests that there is a short time frame after your workout of 15 to 60 minutes in which you must consume protein in order to maximize the effects of your training. But before you rush to grab a protein shake, current research indicates that the anabolic window may not be as important as once believed.

A study investigating this aimed to find the optimal timing and dosage of pre-exercise and post-exercise protein consumption. The results revealed that consuming high amounts of protein either before or after exercise yields maximum anabolic effects [2]. Considering that a resistance training session typically lasts between 45 to 90 minutes, it's also important to ensure that the pre- and post-exercise meals are not separated by more than approximately three to four hours.

Leucine, an essential amino acid, plays a vital role in stimulating signaling pathways for muscle protein synthesis. Studies have consistently shown that a minimum of four grams of leucine is required to maximize protein synthesis. Furthermore, an ideal supplement following resistance exercise should contain whey protein, which provides at least 3 grams of leucine per serving [2].

Proteins are classified as either complete or incomplete. Complete proteins have a complete pairing of amino acids, while incomplete proteins lack one or more amino acids in the sequence. Animal sources of protein, like poultry, eggs, and dairy, are all complete proteins. Plant sources that are complete proteins include quinoa, buckwheat, hempseed, and soybeans.

However, most plant proteins, including tofu, nuts, beans, and rice are incomplete. These protein sources can be combined in meals in order to make them complete, for example beans and rice or pasta and peas. If they are not correctly paired, the body cannot effectively utilize these incomplete proteins for muscle synthesis when they are ingested into the digestive system.

Once you are able to consistently maintain an adequate protein intake, you can then tailor your carbohydrate and fat intake to suit your individual goals and energy requirements.

CARBOHYDRATES

Carbohydrates, or "carbs," are the next most important macronutrient, and they play a vital role in providing energy for our bodies.

Just like a car relies on gasoline to power its engine, carbohydrates serve as the primary fuel source during high-intensity activities, such as sprinting or engaging in quick movements. They provide that quick burst of energy needed to propel us forward, much like how fuel powers a car's acceleration. So, whether it's dashing across the finish line or quickly reacting to unexpected situations, carbohydrates are the dependable energy source that keeps us going strong.

Carbohydrates can be categorized into two types: simple or complex. Complex carbohydrates occur naturally in foods and include sweet potatoes, brown rice, whole wheat, and other fruits and vegetables. These types of carbs offer sustained energy release and provide essential nutrients.

On the other hand, simple carbohydrates are created when complex carbohydrates undergo chemical processing. Examples include breakfast cereals, granola bars, energy drinks, candies, and some ready-to-eat meals. These foods provide a quick energy boost but lack the sustained energy release that complex carbohydrates offer.

The rapid digestion and absorption of simple carbohydrates can lead to a quick energy crash once the initial surge wears off, leaving you feeling tired and sluggish. Not only does the rapid digestion of simple sugars prompt the desire for more sugary foods to maintain energy levels, but it causes a rapid increase in blood sugar levels. This sudden spike results in a surge of insulin, the hormone responsible for regulating blood sugar. Over time, frequent spikes in blood sugar can induce insulin resistance and increase the risk of developing type two diabetes.

Therefore, it is advisable to prioritize complex carbohydrates as the primary source of carbs in your diet. Striking a balance between the types of carbohydrates we consume is crucial for maintaining stable energy levels and supporting overall health.

FATS

When engaging in endurance activities like running, the body is burning both carbohydrates and fats. However, when the fast-burning carbohydrates are completely depleted, fats become the primary fuel source.

Unlike carbohydrates, fats are not a quick source of energy. This delay in energy causes muscles to feel heavy and lethargic. For marathon runners, this phenomenon is commonly known as "hitting the wall," resulting from inadequate carbohydrate availability. To combat this fatigue throughout a race, runners often replenish their energy levels with carbohydrates in the form of sugary drinks or energy gels.

It's important to understand that not all fats are unhealthy or detrimental to performance. The body requires some fats for various essential functions, including hormone production, nutrient absorption, and insulation. A specific form of fat that plays an important role in regulating these processes is cholesterol.

Cholesterol is carried in the bloodstream by lipoproteins, with two main types: low-density lipoprotein (LDL) and high-density lipoprotein (HDL). While cholesterol is necessary for normal body functioning, having excessively high levels of LDL cholesterol can lead to the buildup of plaque in the arteries, increasing the risk of heart disease and other cardiovascular problems. On the other hand, higher levels of HDL cholesterol are associated with a reduced risk of heart disease, as HDL helps transport excess cholesterol away from the arteries.

Choosing the right type of fat is crucial for maintaining a healthy cholesterol profile. Monounsaturated fats and polyunsaturated fats are considered healthy choices as they raise HDL levels in the blood. Foods rich in these fats include nuts, olive oil, flax seeds, avocados, fatty fish, and peanut butter.

Conversely, saturated fats and trans fats are associated with increased LDL levels in the blood, making them unhealthy choices. Foods high in saturated fats include butter, cakes, biscuits, shortening, bacon, cheese, and fried foods. When grocery shopping, it's important to pay attention to nutrition labels as they break down the fat content for you, allowing you to make informed choices about the types and amounts of fats you consume.

As a closing note to our deep dive on the three major macronutrients, I've provided a table of my personal favorite sources from each category. These sources provide a variety of nutrients, flavors, and textures, making them not only nutritionally beneficial, but also enjoyable to incorporate into your meals.

PROTEIN	CARBOHYDRATES	FATS
Egg whites	Brown rice	Avocado
Nonfat Greek yogurt	Rice cakes	Nuts
Tofu	Sweet potatoes	Egg yolk
Salmon	Vegetables	Salmon
Protein powder	Fruits	
Powdered peanut butter	Popcorn	
Beans	Whole wheat tortillas	
Brown rice	Whole grain rolled oats	
Lentils		
Hummus		

THE GUT MICROBIOME

Cravings are often perceived as uncontrollable urges for specific foods, but in reality, they are not some magical force beyond your control. The foods you regularly consume play a significant role in influencing these cravings. This is largely driven by the diverse ecosystem of bacteria residing in your gut collectively known as the gut microbiome.

The gut microbiome is a complex and dynamic environment that consists of trillions of bacteria, fungi, viruses, and other microorganisms. These tiny inhabitants interact with each other and with the cells lining the gut, forming a mutually beneficial relationship that impacts various aspects of our health and well-being.

Although scientists are only scratching the surface of understanding the intricacies of the gut microbiome and its composition, current research suggests a remarkably close connection between the brain and the gut [1]. The communication system—known as the gut-brain axis—allows these two organs to be closely connected, affecting our mood, emotions, and even our cravings for certain foods.

For example, when you consume greasy fast food, you introduce bacteria into your gut that thrive on such foods. Repeatedly indulging in fast food allows these bacteria to thrive, multiplying and occupying more space within your gut.

Consequently, the build-up of fast-food-loving bacteria means there is less room for bacteria that favor nutrient-rich vegetables. Because of the gut-brain axis, an imbalance in favor of greasy, fast food-loving bacteria over vegetable-loving bacteria in your gut can lead to a higher inclination towards craving fast food over vegetables.

On the other hand, when you provide your body with whole grains, fruits, and vegetables, you foster the growth of bacteria in your gut that crave these wholesome foods. This symbiotic relationship between the brain and the gut explains why, when we opt for healthier eating patterns, our cravings align accordingly.

By understanding the intricate connection between the food we eat, the gut microbiome, and our cravings, we can make more informed choices about our dietary habits. Prioritizing a diet rich in diverse whole foods and fiber can help create a healthier gut environment and potentially lead to more balanced and manageable cravings.

CALORIE TRACKING

Being conscious of not only what you're eating, but how much you are eating is an integral aspect to achieving a fitness-related goal. Temporarily tracking your caloric intake will help you gain complete control over your diet and allow you to make informed decisions about your food choices.

Through this practice, you will better understand the energy balance equation, where the calories you consume are compared to the calories you burn. This awareness allows you to adjust your caloric intake according to your specific goals, whether it's weight loss, weight gain, or maintenance.

However, calorie tracking may not be suitable for everyone. For some people, especially those with a history of disordered eating or a tendency to obsess over food and numbers, calorie tracking can trigger negative psychological effects and contribute to an unhealthy relationship with food. In such cases, tracking calories is not recommended.

If you decide to track calories, keep in mind that you should not fixate on calories alone. If you were to only think about calories, you might overlook other essential aspects of nutrition, such as the quality of food choices and the significance of overall nutrient intake. While caloric balance is one factor influencing weight management, the nutritional content of foods, including vitamins, minerals, fiber, and macronutrients is equally important.

Approaching calorie tracking with a balanced mindset means viewing it as a tool rather than an absolute measure of success or failure. Use it as an opportunity to learn more about your dietary patterns, preferences, and hunger cues. In doing so, you are better able to make informed choices that align with your health and wellness goals.

Once you become aware of your dietary habits after tracking for several weeks, you'll be able to gradually transition to practicing intuitive eating, which involves eating when your body signals hunger. However, if you have a specific goal in mind, such as weight management or targeted nutrition, it is advisable to continue tracking your calories for an extended duration. To help, I recommend using MyFitnessPal or LifeSum, as these apps make it easy to track calories and measure progress over time.

By incorporating this practice into your routine, you will develop a better understanding of your nutritional needs as you work towards achieving your health and wellness goals. Ultimately, fostering a healthy relationship with food and adopting positive lifestyle habits will contribute to your long-term success.

SLEEP

While exercise, nutrition, and training are essential components of reaching your fitness goals, they are incomplete without giving due attention to the quality and quantity of your sleep. The recommended amount of sleep is between seven to nine hours for adults and eight to 10 hours for adolescents [19].
One of the primary reasons why sleep is so important is muscle recovery. During deep sleep stages, the body releases growth hormone, which plays a key role in muscle repair. Adequate sleep allows your muscles to heal and rebuild after intense workouts, leading to more muscle gains and reduced risk of injuries.

Additionally, sleep plays a big role in hormonal balance. Lack of sleep can disrupt this balance, leading to decreased muscle mass and increased fat storage, potentially hindering your progress in the gym.

But before you jump straight into bed, keep in mind there are other factors at play, like the timing of your last meal. In order to allow adequate time for your body to completely digest the food you ate for dinner, it's recommended to allow at least two to three hours between your last meal and bedtime.

This was demonstrated in a study in which participants who consumed a meal immediately before bedtime experienced more arousals during the night and had higher blood glucose levels after the meal. This indicates potential disruptions in sleep quality and metabolism [3]. These results were observed because after eating, your body is awake and actively using energy to break down the food you just ate, disrupting your quality of sleep.

Another reason to not lay down right after eating is because gravity will allow the food in your stomach to flow back up your esophagus, also known as acid reflux. While not dangerous if done occasionally, the long-term effects of consistently doing this will result in damage to the walls of the esophagus, as they are not protected against the high-acid content of the stomach.

Establishing a regular sleep schedule is crucial for optimizing your body's natural circadian rhythms. Our bodies have an internal clock that regulates various physiological processes, including sleep-wake cycles. When you adhere to a consistent sleep routine, you align your body with its natural rhythm, promoting better sleep quality and overall well-being.

Ultimately, good sleep is a fundamental pillar of gym performance and overall athletic success. By prioritizing sleep as an integral part of your athletic journey, you set the stage for improved recovery, reduced risk of injuries, and better overall health.

WATER

Water is the driving force of life. Without it, we would not survive more than three days. Thus, the importance of water—especially when it comes to achieving your fitness goals—cannot be overstated. Water helps to maintain nearly every process that occurs in your body, including muscle growth, so inadequate water intake can significantly hinder fitness progress.

As a key component of blood, water is responsible for transporting nutrients, hormones, and other vital substances throughout the body. It also plays an important role in digestion and absorption, which facilitates the conversion of food into energy.

Additionally, the elimination of waste products would not be possible without water. This is because waste is primarily excreted through urine and sweat, which helps detoxify the body and maintain its internal balance. Without sufficient water, these processes become compromised, making it challenging for the body to recover from exercise and properly utilize nutrients. At the end of the day, inadequate water intake can significantly hinder fitness goals.

The optimal amount of water an individual should consume daily can vary depending on several factors, including age, gender, activity level, climate, and health. A commonly recommended guideline is to drink eight cups (64 ounces) of water per day, which is roughly equivalent to two liters or half a gallon. For more active people, however, water needs tend to be higher than the general population, due to increased sweat loss.

This higher water requirement is also due to a higher protein intake, which requires more hydration for proper digestion and metabolic processes. Water helps break down proteins into amino acids, which are then absorbed by the body. Sufficient water intake ensures that the digestive system can efficiently process and absorb the protein consumed.

Proper hydration is crucial for muscle function and recovery. When you're well-hydrated, your muscles can work more efficiently, and this can aid in muscle growth and performance during workouts. Inadequate hydration can lead to decreased exercise performance, muscle cramps, and delayed recovery [8].

A good way to monitor your hydrations levels is to pay attention to the color of your urine; pale yellow urine usually indicates good hydration, while dark yellow or amber urine may indicate the need to drink more water. Keep in mind that individual hydration needs may differ, and it is important to listen to your body's signals of thirst and adjust water intake accordingly.

SUPPLEMENTS

There is no magic solution or shortcut when it comes to weight loss, detoxification, calorie burning, or fat shredding. Frequently, supplement companies are associated with these magical solutions, using words like "quick," "easy," and "fast" to entice susceptible victims and cause them to spend money on illegitimate products. Unfortunately, these deceptive practices are common in the multibillion-dollar supplement industry.

However, proper supplementation can play a beneficial role in fitness progress. The key lies in having a solid understanding of science-backed supplements and their benefits. By being informed and discerning, you can navigate are able to vast array of products and make wise choices based on reliable research.

This next section will take you through an in-depth exploration of the widely employed supplements in the fitness industry. Armed with this knowledge, you will be equipped to make confident and informed decisions about the supplements that truly align with your unique needs and goals.

PROTEIN POWDER

Protein powder stands as one of the most widely utilized fitness supplements among those striving to meet their nutritional needs. While protein is naturally present in various foods, many people struggle to consume sufficient amounts through their diet. Hence, incorporating a protein supplement can be helpful in attaining the recommended daily intake.

While it can be a convenient aid in reaching your protein goal, it's advised to limit protein powder consumption to approximately one serving per day. This is because the quality of protein in powder form is not as high as that found naturally in whole foods. Moreover, it's worth noting that protein powders often contain processed ingredients like artificial sugars and chemicals, which enhance taste and solubility. To maximize the benefits of your protein consumption, prioritize natural food sources like meats, dairy products, legumes, and rice, which provide wholesome and high-quality protein.

The timing of protein intake has been a subject of debate. Some believe that it should be consumed within one hour of your workout for best absorption and results, but research indicates that the specific timing does not significantly impact muscle gains [2].

Rather, the key lies in achieving your daily protein goal, regardless of the specific timing of when you consume it. Prioritizing overall protein intake allows for more flexibility in meal planning and makes it easier to maintain a balanced and sustainable diet.

CREATINE

Creatine is a naturally occurring organic compound that can be found in various tissues of the human body, including the heart, brain, and muscles. Its primary function is to assist in the production of energy in the form of adenosine triphosphate (ATP). The greater the availability of ATP, the more capacity for physical exertion and the greater the ability to handle heavier loads during your lifting session.

While it is possible to obtain creatine through dietary sources such as milk, red meat, and seafood, relying solely on these foods can have drawbacks. If consumed in excess, concerns related to cholesterol and other negative effects can arise. A more convenient and controlled method of intake for creatine is through supplementation.

The most prevalent and cost-effective form of creatine is creatine monohydrate, produced by combining creatine with a single water molecule, which is why it is referred to as "mono" meaning "one," and "hydrate" meaning "water." Creatine is also a common primary ingredient in pre-workout supplements.

The recommended dosage of creatine to maximize its effects on muscular gains is five grams per day. Taking this amount consistently every day, even on non-workout days, will ensure a continuous supply of creatine in the body.

Exceeding the five-gram threshold has not demonstrated any additional benefits in terms of muscle development [9]. Nonetheless, incorporating creatine supplementation into your regimen can prove to be a valuable tool in unlocking your maximum potential.

PRE-WORKOUT

Pre-workout is a flavored powder that, when mixed with water, creates a drink similar to Gatorade. However, unlike Gatorade and other sports drinks, the primary ingredients in pre-workout supplements are designed to stimulate your senses and heighten your awareness. Understanding the most common ingredients and their effects will help you determine if pre-workout is for you.

The most common ingredient in pre-workout supplements is caffeine. This is because caffeine has been shown to increase muscle strength and output during exercise while reducing fatigue [17]. In other words, caffeine can help you get the most out of your workout.

However, caffeine has some negative side effects if overconsumed, such as insomnia, nausea, increased heart rate, headaches, anxiety, and jitteriness. It's easy to overconsume caffeine by drinking pre-workout, as they typically have approximately 500mg of caffeine per serving. To compare, a cup of coffee (240mL) has 95 mg of caffeine, nearly one fifth the amount. This significant disparity highlights the potential for unwanted side effects associated with pre-workout consumption.

Creatine has been proven to increase high intensity exercise capacity and lean body mass gains from exercise. No other side effects, such as digestive issues, dehydration, or muscle cramps have been confirmed in clinical studies with creatine [9].

Beta alanine is an amino acid that reduces acidity in your muscles while exercising. This helps sustain a workout for slightly longer. When dosed at four to six grams, beta alanine has been shown to increase exercise performance and reduce fatigue in high intensity exercise. At the same time, this ingredient can cause paresthesia, which is a tingling sensation in your hands and feet. It's harmless, but many people find it uncomfortable.

Niacin, or vitamin B3, plays an important role in energy metabolism by helping the body produce energy from food. It can also help with muscle growth and recovery. The average serving of pre-workout has about 25.8mg of niacin and may contain up to 41mg [7]. For reference, the daily recommended amount of niacin is 16mg for men and 14mg for women. When you go beyond the recommended dosage, niacin triggers blood vessel dilation, which may cause flushing of the skin. The thing is, niacin is found in food naturally, so if you eat a well-balanced diet, supplementation will likely not offer any benefits other than red skin.

Citrulline is an amino acid meant to increase blood flow to muscles during exercise, which results in an increased rate of muscle building. It's important to note that the increased blood flow from citrulline will affect the brain as well as muscle. With that said, it is not uncommon for some people to experience headaches or migraines as a result of the blood pressure changes in the brain's small blood vessels.

In addition to the more familiar ingredients, there exists a wide array of artificial sugars, gums, thickening agents, colorizers, and chemicals that are incorporated to enhance flavor. Many of these additives, such as aspartame and erythritol, have not undergone extensive research and their long-term effects remain uncertain due to their relatively short presence in the market.

Due to this lack of clarity, I personally choose to err on the side of caution and avoid the use of pre-workout supplements. Whenever I find myself in need of an energy boost, a simple cup of black coffee with a dash of almond milk has always sufficed for me, and I believe it can provide all the necessary stimulation for anyone.

Indeed, all supplements have the potential to provide various benefits and drawbacks. While some supplements can have positive effects when used appropriately, not all products are equally effective or safe for everyone. Follow the recommended dosage instructions on the supplement's packaging or as advised by your healthcare professional. "More" is not always better when it comes to supplements, and overconsumption can be harmful to your health.

Additionally, the supplement industry is vast, and not all products undergo rigorous testing or regulation. Be wary of extravagant claims or promises made by supplement manufacturers. Seek out reputable brands with transparent ingredient lists and third-party testing to ensure the product's quality and safety.

Remember that supplements should complement a well-balanced and nutritious diet, not replace it. Maintaining a balanced perspective will help you make informed choices and maximize the potential benefits of supplements while safeguarding your overall well-being.

NICKI BRIGHT

10 FAD DIETS AND THE ONLY DIET YOU SHOULD BE ON

From the popular keto diet to the Atkins plan, and from the vegan lifestyles to the plant-powered word of vegetarianism, the options seem endless. Each diet claims to possess the magic formula for attaining the body of your dreams.

The prevalence of these various diet trends has led to a distortion in humanity's perception of health and nutrition. Many people find themselves constantly searching for the "perfect" diet that will magically transform their bodies, and they may hop from one diet to another in pursuit of quick results. However, this approach can be misleading.

Let's take, for example, the lemon water trend. A quick search on the internet reveals claims that drinking lemon water improves digestion, rids the body of toxins, has antimicrobial properties, aids in weight loss, and is good for your skin.

These purported benefits are not solely attributable to lemons themselves. In reality, drinking water, whether with or without lemons, can indeed aid in digestion and potentially assist with weight loss. There is little to no research supporting the notion that adding lemon juice to water can effectively detoxify the body or induce weight loss [16]. Yet somewhere along the way, the idea has gained traction through the influence of celebrities and social media influencers who promote it as a miracle health solution.

Think about it. If lemons were the answer to weight loss, the demand for lemons would skyrocket and they would be growing on every hillside. However, the reality is that lemon trees are not more commonly grown than any other fruit. This begs the question: can lemons really be the secret to weight loss?

The point I'm trying to emphasize is that we should not fall victim to advertising tactics. Companies target those who are vulnerable and desperate—those who are willing to believe even the most far-fetched claims. True fitness freedom lies in being able to discern between evidence-based practices and the latest dieting trends. Rather than relying on catchy slogans or celebrity endorsements, invest time in gaining knowledge. Understand nutrition, exercise science, and the unique needs of your body, for only then will you be able to discern between short-lived trends and long-term habits. In doing so, we avoid repeating the mistakes of past dieting trends.

THE LOW-FAT DIET

A prevailing belief in the 1990s was that eating fat equated to gaining fat. This gave rise to low-fat and fat-free diets.

One of the primary concerns with a low-fat or fat-free diet is the potential deficiency in essential nutrients. Not all fats are detrimental and eliminating them entirely can adversely affect one's overall health. Dietary fats are a primary source of essential fatty acids, such as omega-three and omega-six fatty acids. These fats play a crucial role in various bodily functions, including brain health, hormone production, and inflammation regulation. By avoiding fats, you deprive your body of these nutrients, leading to potential deficiencies and related health issues.

Another concern with low-fat diets is related to satiety and hunger management. Fats provide a sense of fullness and satisfaction after meals, which can help regulate appetite and prevent overeating. When you eliminate fats from your diet, you may find yourself feeling less satisfied after meals, leading to increased hunger and a higher likelihood of reaching for unhealthy snacks to curb your cravings.

Additionally, in order to compensate for the lack of flavor and texture that fats provide, low-fat or fat-free processed foods usually contain higher amounts of added sugars, refined carbohydrates, and artificial ingredients. In essence, low-fat diets simply replaced one food group with others. Not only that, but the additives used to improve flavor increased the calorie content. This contributed to potential health issues like weight gain, dental problems, and metabolic imbalances.

Despite the diligent effort directed towards avoiding fat, people on these diets experienced minimal weight loss. In fact, the lack of satiety experienced with the low-fat diet often resulted in weight gain. Many seekers of a healthier lifestyle were left with no choice but to shift their attention to the next fad diet on the horizon.

THE ATKINS DIET

During the early 2000s, a new dietary approach gained popularity: the Atkins diet. After years of being deprived of cheese and bacon, it came as no surprise that a diet that permitted the consumption of these foods was warmly welcomed.

The core principle of this diet was to restrict carbohydrates and replace them with increased consumption of fats and proteins. The diet consists of four phases, starting with a very low-carb induction phase, around 40 grams per day, and gradually increasing carbohydrate intake as the person progresses. The diet plateaus at its fourth phase, the "maintenance" phase, in which the person is expected to eat only 80 to 100 grams of carbohydrates every day for the rest of their life.

As a point of reference, Dietary Guidelines for Americans recommend that carbohydrates make up 45% to 65% of total daily calories [11]. That means that if you eat 2,000 calories, you should be eating between 225 and 325 grams of carbohydrates. The Atkins diet falls considerably short of these recommended numbers, even during its maintenance phase. This raises the question of whether it is genuinely sustainable in the long term.

Furthermore, by focusing solely on hitting those low carbohydrate numbers, the Atkins diet is deficient of the essential nutrients provided by carbohydrate sources like whole grains and fruits. As a result, energy levels, metabolism, and overall health may become compromised.

On top that, the restrictive nature of the Atkins diet makes it challenging to maintain over time. This led to frustration and potential overconsumption of carbohydrates once a regular diet resumed. The cycle of restriction and overeating hindered long-term weight loss efforts, making the search for the perfect diet continue.

THE KETO DIET

The current dietary fad is the keto diet. While both the Atkins and keto diet emphasize a reduction in carbohydrates, the degree of restriction differs. The keto diet takes a more extreme approach, allowing only 20 to 50 grams of carbohydrates each day. There are no phases or gradual increases.

The state of carbohydrate depletion caused by consuming this little amount of carbohydrates is called "ketosis." This occurs when ketone molecules are produced by the liver from fatty acids in the absence of sufficient carbohydrates. The energy produced by ketones is used to support muscles, the brain, and other tissues. In essence, following a keto diet convinces the body to act metabolically as if its starving, even though it isn't.

Interestingly, the keto diet traces back to the 1920s, in which it was originally used as a treatment for epilepsy. Fasting was known to have anti-seizure effects, so the diet was designed to mimic starvation. With the development of new antiepileptic drugs, the use of the keto diet for epilepsy treatment has declined and instead, is more popularly used for its potential to aid in weight loss.

The weight loss success that some people have experienced on this diet is attributed to the fact that cutting out a major food group makes it easier to be in a caloric deficit. However, the macronutrient imbalance and high intake of fats can have adverse effects on heart health.

While some proponents of the diet emphasize the consumption of healthy fats like avocados and nuts, it's not uncommon for people to consume unhealthy fats from processed and fried foods on the diet. High intake of saturated fats, such as fatty meat, full-fat dairy products, and added oils like butter and coconut oil, has been consistently linked to an increased risk of heart disease and elevated levels of LDL cholesterol (commonly referred to as "bad cholesterol") [13].

Due to these challenges and health concerns, the keto diet is considered unsustainable in the long term. As a result, those looking to find a long-lasting approach to nutrition may seek alternative diets.

However, what many of these diets fail to address is the fundamental principle of weight management: calories in versus calories out. Regardless of the source of calories—whether from carbohydrates, fats, or proteins—

consuming more calories than the body burns will lead to weight gain. This principle applies universally, regardless of the specific diet followed.

For example, a person following a vegan or vegetarian diet, which is often associated with healthier food choices, can still experience weight gain if they overconsume calories. While plant-based diets may offer numerous health benefits, the importance of portion control and mindful eating cannot be overlooked. Without a focus on overall caloric intake, any diet, no matter how "healthy" it appears, may not be effective in achieving weight loss goals.

Keep in mind that different types of foods have varying effects on hunger, satiety, metabolism, and overall health. For example, a diet rich in whole, nutrient-dense foods like vegetables, fruits, whole grains, lean proteins, and healthy fats can promote better health, provide essential nutrients, and support weight management due to their fiber content and nutrient density. On the other hand, diets high in processed foods, added sugars, and unhealthy fats may be less satisfying and can lead to overeating and weight gain.

Upon closer observation of the fad diets mentioned, a recurring pattern emerges: the elimination of a specific macronutrient only to be replaced by another. Thus, you can see why these diets would render ineffective for weight loss, as the person is likely still consuming an excess of calories. Moreover, by depriving the body of essential nutrients and vitamins, such diets can adversely affect the proper functioning of tissues and organs, especially when adhered to for extended periods of time.

The allure of quick and promising weight loss results can be tempting, but the reality is usually disappointing. Fad diets typically fail to deliver sustainable and lasting weight loss, leaving individuals feeling frustrated and disheartened. The pursuit of fitness freedom is a journey, not a quick fix.

A sustainable diet is one that you can comfortably maintain for the long term, promoting not only physical health but also mental and emotional well-being. When you embrace a balanced and sustainable approach to nutrition, you'll discover that there is only one diet that will truly support you in achieving a healthier and happier life.

THE ONLY DIET YOU SHOULD BE ON

While it's true that certain diets may offer benefits to people with specific deficiencies or health concerns, there is only one dietary approach that can reliably provide all necessary vitamins and nutrients while also being sustainable. This is the diet of variety.

A diet of variety eliminates the need for dietary restrictions or the exclusion of entire food groups. Instead, it allows occasional indulgences, as long as the overall dietary pattern remains focused on the criteria of balance and diversity. This not only honors the body's natural cravings, but fosters a healthy, well-rounded relationship with food that will last a lifetime.

One of the key priorities in your diet should be emphasizing protein intake, as it is the fundamental building block for muscle development and repair. By prioritizing protein-rich foods, you provide your body with the necessary nutrients to support muscle growth and recovery.

Additionally, limiting the amount of processed foods should be a priority. Processed foods often contain high levels of unhealthy fats and added sugars, which can contribute to excess calories and hinder your progress in achieving your nutritional goals. By minimizing your intake of such foods, you direct your body's focus towards promoting muscle growth and fat loss.

If you find it challenging to maintain a healthy diet, take a minute to evaluate the contents of your fridge and pantry at home. Finding an abundance of processed foods is a clear indication that your shopping habits need to change. You set yourself up for success when you only allow only healthy foods in your kitchen. Bringing home items that don't align with your goals only undermines your efforts to eat healthier.

A trick to ensure that only healthy foods enter your home is to do most of your shopping around the perimeter of the grocery store. You'll find that the perimeter of the store includes the fresh produce, eggs, dairy products, meats, and whole grains. The middle of the store is where most processed foods reside, in the isles abundant with candy, chips, ice cream, cereals, and pre-packaged meals. By avoiding these inner aisles, where tempting processed foods lurk, you create a physical boundary that helps resist the allure of less nutritious choices. This deliberate shopping technique makes it so that the next time you are looking for a quick snack at home, you stay focused on your health goals.

Another important habit to adopt is being skeptical. In today's digital age, misinformation spreads rapidly through social media and other platforms. Don't blindly follow what everyone else is doing simply because of an advertisement or celebrity endorsement. Fad diets, in particular, make grandiose promises of transforming your physique, but upon closer examination of their sources, these claims lack credibility. To become a more informed reader, prioritize reputable and well-established publications, peer-reviewed studies, and insights from experts in the relevant field.

A crucial aspect of being an informed reader is to be aware of potential biases and agendas that may influence the presentation of information. Be mindful of the author's affiliations, potential conflicts of interest, and the overall tone of the content. Balanced and unbiased reporting should be sought, allowing for a comprehensive understanding of the topic. Moreover, cross-referencing information from various sources aids in confirming its accuracy and shields you from falling prey to misinformation or biased narratives.

Ultimately, the key is to maintain a mindful and informed approach to food choices, ensuring that your diet encompasses a little bit of everything in moderation. By adopting a diet of variety, only bringing healthy choices into your home, and being a skeptic when it comes to new fad diets, you will find satisfaction, enjoyment, and long-term success.

RESTAURANTS

Frequently eating at restaurants can be detrimental to your health. This is because the food industry usually prioritizes taste over nutritional value and disregards the excessive levels of sugar, sodium, fat, and calories.

Thus, restaurant visits should be limited. Save dining out for special occasions or when you can enjoy social interactions with friends and loved ones. On such occasions, the experience of sharing a meal can be deeply fulfilling and enjoyable. However, when eating out lacks the element of social connection, it's wise to prioritize cooking the majority of your meals at home.

Cooking at home grants you the invaluable opportunity to take charge of your health and well-being. You gain complete control over the ingredients used, portion sizes, and cooking methods. This control empowers you to incorporate an abundance of fresh, whole foods and minimize the consumption of processed and unhealthy options. This practice also leads to cost savings and a reduced environmental footprint, as you minimize the reliance on disposable packaging and processed foods.

When you choose to dine out, it's even more essential to take proactive measures in choosing nutritious meals. Take the time to carefully review the menu, paying attention to the available options and their ingredients. If a nutritional guide is provided, make use of it to gather valuable information about the meals. By becoming a proactive guardian of your well-being, you can make informed choices that align with your health goals. Remember, even in a restaurant setting, you have the power to prioritize your health and make decisions that support your fitness goals.

In those situations where fast food is your only available choice, you should consider ordering a light meal or snack in order to hold you over until you have access to other more nutritious, satiating options. For your convenience, I've compiled a list of relatively healthier menu options from popular fast-food chains.

It's worth noting that while these choices may be considered healthier compared to other items on the menus, fast food should generally be consumed sparingly to maintain balance within your overall diet. By being mindful of your selections, you can make the most out of these situations without compromising your commitment to your health.

IN-N-OUT BURGER
Protein Style Burger
Calories: Around 240-270 calories
Protein: Around 18-20 grams

CHICK-FIL-A
Grilled Chicken Sandwich
Calories: Around 320 calories
Protein: Around 29 grams

TACO BELL
Power Menu Bowl (with grilled chicken or steak)
Calories: Around 490-500 calories
Protein: Around 20-30 grams

Fresco Soft Tacos (chicken or beef)
Calories: Around 140-160 calories per taco
Protein: Around 10-12 grams per taco

Black Bean Burrito
Calories: Around 380-400 calories
Protein: Around 12-14 grams

MCDONALD'S
Grilled Chicken Sandwich (without sauce)
Calories: Around 380-400 calories
Protein: Around 36 grams

Egg White Delight McMuffin
Calories: Around 250-280 calories
Protein: Around 17-19 grams

SUBWAY
Turkey Breast Sandwich (on whole wheat bread, loaded with vegetables)
Calories: Around 300-350 calories
Protein: Around 20-25 grams

Veggie Delite Sandwich (on whole wheat bread, loaded with vegetables)
Calories: Around 230-280 calories
Protein: Around 6-8 grams

Rotisserie-Style Chicken Salad
Calories: Around 210-250 calories
Protein: Around 30-35 grams

Fresh Fit Chopped Salad (with lean protein options like turkey or chicken)
Calories: Around 150-300 calories (depending on toppings and dressings)
Protein: Around 10-20 grams

CARL'S JR
Charbroiled Chicken Salad
Calories: Around 200-250 calories
Protein: Around 20-30 grams

Original Grilled Chicken Sandwich
Calories: Around 350-400 calories
Protein: Around 25-30 grams

Turkey Burger (without sauce)
Calories: Around 300-350 calories
Protein: Around 20-25 grams

Low-Carb Thickburger (lettuce wrapped)
Calories: Around 500-600 calories
Protein: Around 25-30 grams

JACK IN THE BOX
Grilled Chicken Salad (with lighter dressings like balsamic vinaigrette)
Calories: Around 200-250 calories
Protein: Around 25-30 grams

Grilled Chicken Strips
Calories: Around 200-250 calories (for 4 strips)
Protein: Around 20-25 grams (for 4 strips)

Chicken Fajita Pita (without sauce)
Calories: Around 250-300 calories
Protein: Around 15-20 grams

STARBUCKS
Egg White Feta Wrap
Calories: Around 230-280 calories
Protein: Around 13-19 grams

Egg White Bites
Calories: Around 170-190 calories (for 2 bites)
Protein: Around 13-15 grams (for 2 bites)

Oatmeal
Calories: Around 160-210 calories (depending on flavor and toppings)
Protein: Around 4-6 grams

Please note that the specific calorie count may vary based on the size of the drink and the specific ingredients used. It's always a good idea to check the restaurant's website or consult their nutrition information for more accurate details. Additionally, customization and portion control can play a significant role in making these choices healthier.

LIQUID CALORIES

A common habit that most people don't even realize they are doing is drinking their calories instead of consuming them. Liquid calories are often devoid of nutritional value and packed with excess calories. Beverages such as alcohol, sugary coffee drinks, and soda are prime examples, as they frequently contain high amounts of sugar and fats, contributing to their calorie-dense nature.

Take, for instance, the specialty s'mores Frappuccino from Starbucks is a 16-ounce drink that packs a staggering 490 calories and a hefty 67 grams of sugar. Considering the recommended daily added sugar intake of 36 grams for men and 25 grams for women, a single morning coffee can easily exceed the entire day's allotted sugar intake. Moreover, those 500 calories consumed from such beverages offer little in the way of protein, which is essential for muscle growth and development.

The question arises: Why even consume these calorie-laden beverages in the first place? They offer little nutritional benefit, and instead make up a significant portion your overall caloric intake and potentially hindering your fitness and health goals.

Considering the detrimental effects of liquid calories on our nutrition and overall well-being, it becomes imperative to prioritize healthy eating habits and make conscious choices regarding what we consume.

SMALL BITES, BIG IMPACT

Often, people underestimate the impact of small bites, nibbles, and sips throughout the day, failing to realize how quickly these small indulgences can add up and steer them away from their fitness goals.

The key is to keep only snacks that align with your fitness goals within easy reach. Whether it's at home, in your pantry, in your car, or even at work, having high-protein snacks readily available ensures that you'll opt for those when you're craving something quick and tasty.

Adopting a habit of choosing protein-rich snacks is a game-changer. Instead of consuming excess calories that set you back, these snacks contribute to reaching your daily protein target. As a general guideline, aim for snacks that provide at least one gram of protein for every 10 calories.

By incorporating this approach, you're effectively using every calorie, no matter how seemingly insignificant, to support your goals, keeping you on track and satisfied. With options like protein bars, nonfat Greek yogurt parfaits, chocolate protein powder smoothies, and various combinations of protein-packed ingredients, you have a wide range of delicious and nutritious choices to enjoy while still making progress and feeling energized.

In the journey towards finding fitness freedom, the significance of embracing small steps cannot be overstated. Each seemingly insignificant choice to prioritize movement, make healthier food choices, and practice self-care accumulates into a transformative and empowering lifestyle.

By focusing on incremental progress and celebrating every victory, no matter how small, we build the foundation for sustainable change and long-term success. These small steps not only shape our physical well-being, but also foster mental resilience and self-confidence, propelling us towards achieving our fitness goals and ultimately finding true freedom in living a healthy and fulfilling life.

MAIN MUSCLE GROUPS

Although we all have a body, many of us lack a comprehensive understanding of its functional capabilities. The human body is an intricate masterpiece, composed of complex systems and processes that never cease to amaze me.

My degree in biology serves as a testament to my deep passion for understanding anatomy. I immediately recognized its potential to enhance my comprehension of exercise and improve my progress in the gym. Understanding anatomy empowered me to make educated decisions about training techniques, target specific muscle groups more effectively, and comprehend the physiological changes occurring within my body as a result of exercise.

Although delving into the captivating complexities of the human body is not necessary for everyone, having a basic grasp of muscular anatomy remains a crucial cornerstone in your fitness journey. By familiarizing yourself with the major muscle groups in your body, you lay the groundwork for establishing a powerful mind-muscle connection, allowing you to fully engage and activate specific muscles during exercises. It enables you to direct your focus, concentration, and intention towards the targeted muscle groups, optimizing their recruitment and ultimately enhancing your performance.

In the following section, I have made an outline of the main muscle groups you should become familiar with. This understanding allows you to target specific muscle groups effectively, design well-rounded training routines, and adapt your approach as you progress on your fitness journey.

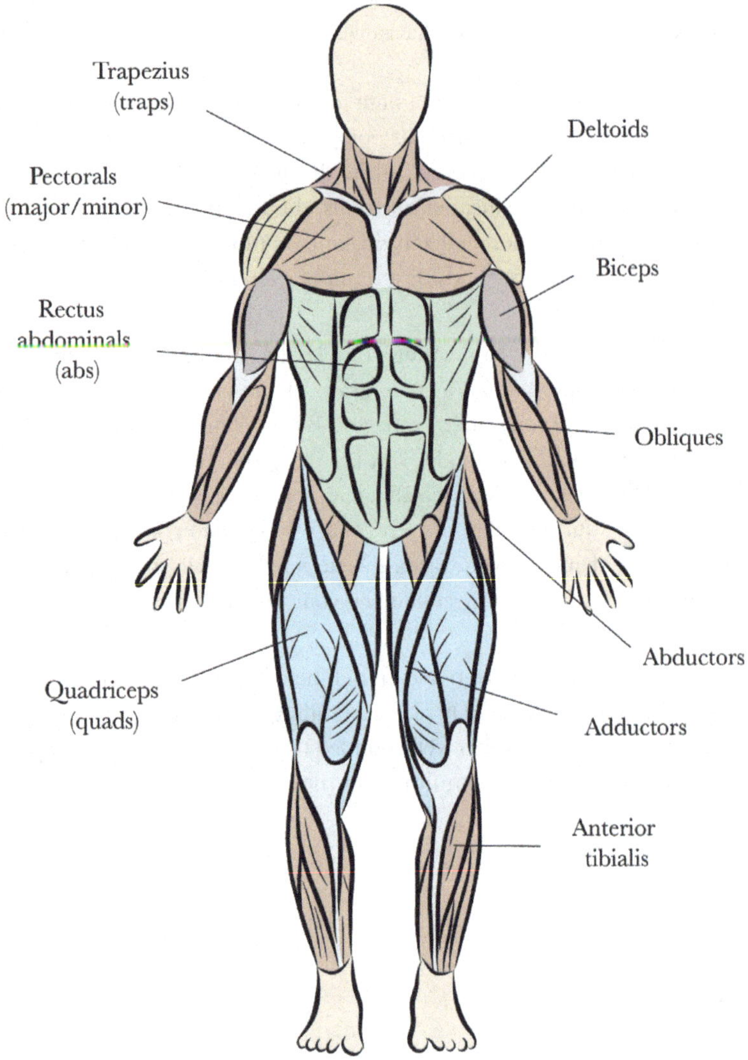
Trapezius
(traps)
Pectorals
(major/minor)
Rectus
abdominals
(abs)
Quadriceps
(quads)
Deltoids
Biceps
Obliques
Abductors
Adductors
Anterior
tibialis

Rhomboids

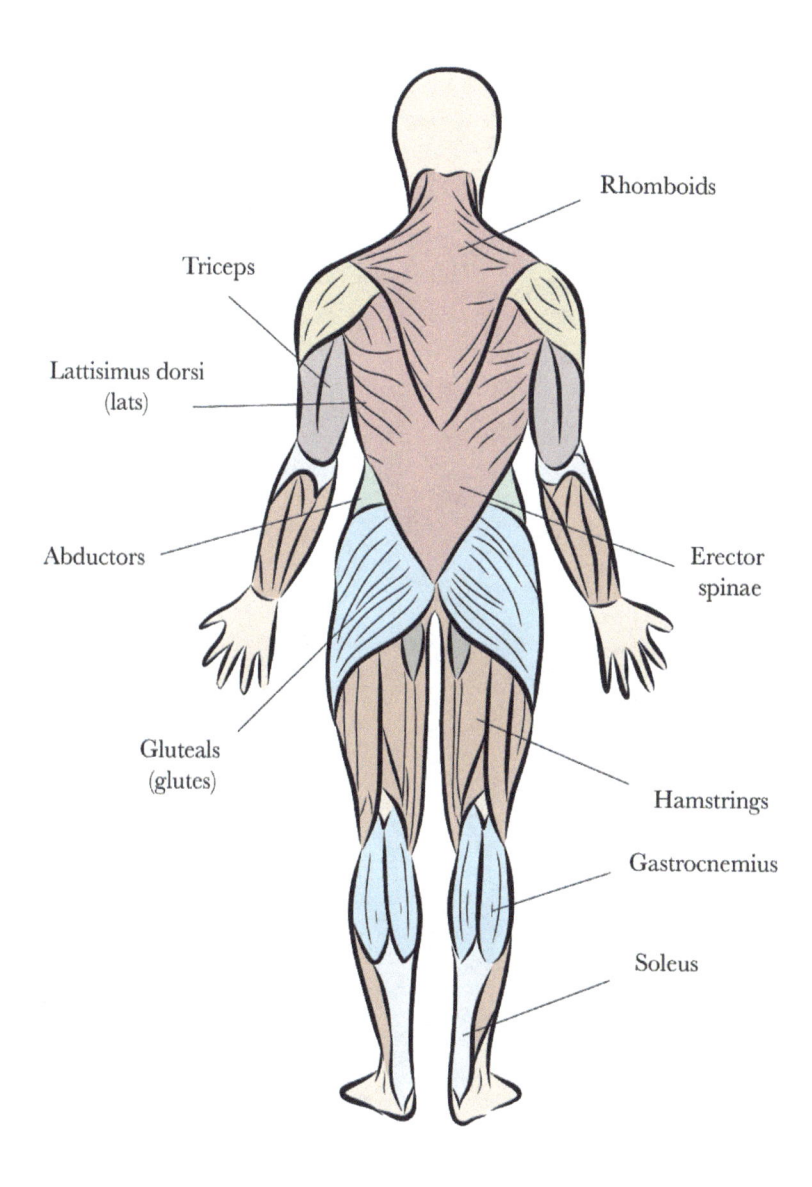

Triceps

Lattisimus dorsi
(lats)

Abductors

Gluteals
(glutes)

Erector
spinae

Hamstrings

Gastrocnemius

Soleus

GLOSSARY OF WEIGHTLIFTING TERMS

AMRAP: Abbreviation for "as many reps as possible;" similar to failure, indicating reps to be performed until the muscles are so fatigued they cannot perform another rep with proper form.

Anabolism: A metabolic process that leads to molecular growth. Muscle mass increases when one is in an anabolic state, with contributing hormones like testosterone, insulin, and human growth hormone.

ATP: Abbreviation for "adenosine triphosphate"; the body's energy system. ATP is an enzyme responsible for transporting energy in all cellular processes in the body, including muscle contraction. The more ATP one has, the better they will be at processing ATP, resulting in more strength. Strength training increases the muscle cell's ability to store more ATP and increases the number of enzymes required for ATP production.

Catabolism: A metabolic process that leads to molecular breakdown. Muscle mass decreases when one is in a catabolic state, with contributing hormones like cortisol and adrenaline.

Compound Exercises: Exercises that involve more than one muscle group and joint. Examples of compound exercises are bench press, deadlifts, pull-ups, push-ups, and squats.

Concentric Contraction: The contraction of a muscle; also known as the shortening of a muscle. As an example, a concentric contraction during a bicep curl is when the dumbbell is brought up towards your body.

Eccentric Contraction: The relaxation of a muscle; also known as the lengthening of a muscle. As an example, an eccentric contraction during a bicep curl is when the dumbbell is lowered back down to the starting position.

Failure: The point at which an individual's muscles are so fatigued during exercise that they can't do any more reps with proper form.

Isolation Exercises: Exercises that involve one joint and a small amount of muscle groups. Examples of isolation exercises are bicep curls, hamstring curls, and tricep extensions.

Isometric Contraction: The contraction of a muscle without movement. As an example, an isometric contraction during a bicep curl is when the dumbbell is at the end of the concentric contraction at the top of the movement.

PR (or PB): Abbreviation for "Personal Record" or "Personal Best"; an individual's best attempt at completing a task, such as their highest weight lifted, longest distance run, or most number of reps completed.

Rate of Perceived Exertion (RPE): A 0-10 measurement of how hard an exercise feels for the lifter. RPE should be between 6-10 for weight training.

Repetition (rep): The amount of times a weight is lifted and lowered in one set of an exercise.

Set: A group of reps. If a workout calls for 3 sets of 12 reps (3x12), then there are 12 reps of the lift for each set followed by a rest period. After the rest period, then you move on to the next set of 12 reps, rest, and repeat once more.

Superset: Two exercises performed back-to-back with no rest between sets. Rest period usually comes after the superset is completed. The exercises can either target the same muscle group, opposing muscle groups, or be unrelated.

Tempo: The speed at which a rep is performed, including the concentric, isometric, and eccentric contraction. The tempo that allows for full control of the weight with no momentum is a fast (1 second) concentric contraction and a slow (3-4 second) eccentric contraction.

Volume: Usually determined by how many sets, reps, and exercises are completed and is a way to measure the intensity of a workout.

Weight: The amount of resistance that is being lifted.

REFERENCES

1. Carabotti M, Scirocco A, Maselli MA, Severi C. The gut-brain axis: interactions between enteric microbiota, central and enteric nervous systems. Ann Gastroenterol. 2015 Apr-Jun;28(2):203-209. PMID: 25830558; PMCID: PMC4367209.
2. Cintineo, H. P., Arent, M. A., Antonio, J., & Arent, S. M. (2018, September 11). "Effects of protein supplementation on performance and recovery in resistance and endurance training." Frontiers in nutrition. Retrieved June 1, 2022.
3. Crispim CA, Zimberg IZ, dos Reis BG, Diniz RM, Tufik S, de Mello MT. Relationship between food intake and sleep pattern in healthy individuals. J Clin Sleep Med. 2011 Dec 15;7(6):659-64. doi: 10.5664/jcsm.1476. PMID: 22171206; PMCID: PMC3227713.
4. de Salles BF, Simão R, Miranda F, Novaes Jda S, Lemos A, Willardson JM. Rest interval between sets in strength training. Sports Med. 2009;39(9):765-77. doi: 10.2165/11315230-000000000-00000. PMID: 19691365.
5. Foley D, Ancoli-Israel S, Britz P, Walsh J. Sleep disturbances and chronic disease in older adults: results of the 2003 National Sleep Foundation Sleep in America Survey. J Psychosom Res. 2004 May;56(5):497-502. doi:10.1016/j.jpsychores.2004.02.010. PMID: 15172205.
6. Janse de Jonge XA. Effects of the menstrual cycle on exercise performance. Sports Med. 2003;33(11):833-51. doi: 10.2165/00007256-200333110-00004. PMID: 12959622.
7. Jagim AR, Harty PS, Camic CL. Common Ingredient Profiles of Multi-Ingredient Pre-Workout Supplements. Nutrients. 2019 Jan 24;11(2):254. doi: 10.3390/nu11020254. PMID: 30678328; PMCID: PMC6413194.
8. Judelson, D. A., Maresh, C. M., Farrell, M. J., Yamamoto, L., Armstrong, L., Kraemer, W., Volek, J., Spiering, B., Casa, D., & Anderson, J. (2007, October). Effect of hydration state on strength, power, and... : Medicine & Science in Sports & Exercise. Medicine and Science in Sports and Exercise.
9. Kreider RB, Kalman DS, Antonio J, Ziegenfuss TN, Wildman R, Collins R, Candow DG, Kleiner SM, Almada AL, Lopez HL. International Society of Sports Nutrition position stand: safety and efficacy of

creatine supplementation in exercise, sport, and medicine. J Int Soc Sports Nutr. 2017 Jun 13;14:18. doi: 10.1186/s12970-017-0173-z. PMID: 28615996; PMCID: PMC5469049.
10. Manske SL, Lorincz CR, Zernicke RF. Bone health: part 2, physical activity. Sports Health. 2009 Jul;1(4):341-6. doi: 10.1177/1941738109338823. PMID: 23015892; PMCID: PMC3445123.
11. Mayo Foundation for Medical Education and Research. (2022, March 22). Choose your Carbs wisely. Mayo Clinic.
12. Page P. Current concepts in muscle stretching for exercise and rehabilitation. Int J Sports Phys Ther. 2012 Feb;7(1):109-19. PMID: 22319684; PMCID: PMC3273886.
13. Siri-Tarino PW, Sun Q, Hu FB, Krauss RM. Meta-analysis of prospective cohort studies evaluating the association of saturated fat with cardiovascular disease. Am J Clin Nutr. 2010 Mar;91(3):535-46. doi: 10.3945/ajcn.2009.27725. Epub 2010 Jan 13. PMID: 20071648; PMCID: PMC2824152.
14. Slimani M, Tod D, Chaabene H, Miarka B, Chamari K. Effects of Mental Imagery on Muscular Strength in Healthy and Patient Participants: A Systematic Review. J Sports Sci Med. 2016 Aug 5;15(3):434-450. PMID: 27803622; PMCID: PMC4974856.
15. Stutz, J., Eiholzer, R., & Spengler, C. M. (2018). Effects of evening exercise on sleep in healthy participants: A systematic review and meta-analysis. Sports Medicine, 49(2), 269–287.
16. U.S. Department of Health and Human Services. (2019, September). "Detoxes" and "cleanses": What you need to know. National Center for Complementary and Integrative Health.
17. VanDusseldorp TA, Guest NS, Nelson MT, Grgic J, Schoenfeld BJ, Jenkins NDM, Arent SM, Antonio J, Stout JR, Trexler ET, Smith-Ryan AE, Goldstein ER, Kalman DS, Campbell BI. International society of sports nutrition position stand: caffeine and exercise performance. J Int Soc Sports Nutr. 2021 Jan 2;18(1):1. doi: 10.1186/s12970-020-00383-4. PMID: 33388079; PMCID: PMC7777221.
18. Vingren JL, Kraemer WJ, Ratamess NA, Anderson JM, Volek JS, Maresh CM. Testosterone physiology in resistance exercise and training: the up-stream regulatory elements. Sports Med. 2010 Dec 1;40(12):1037-53. doi: 10.2165/11536910-000000000-00000. PMID: 21058750.

19. Watson, Andrew M. MD, MS. Sleep and Athletic Performance. Current Sports Medicine Reports 16(6):p 413-418, 11/12 2017. | DOI: 10.1249/JSR.0000000000000418
20. Winters-Stone KM, Snow CM. Site-specific response of bone to exercise in premenopausal women. Bone. 2006; 39(6): 1203-1209.

ADDITIONAL READING

Bhaskar, S., Hemavathy, D., & Prasad, S. (2016). "Prevalence of chronic insomnia in adult patients and its correlation with medical comorbidities." Journal of family medicine and primary care.

Boldt, A. "Can too much exercise and a lack of calories cause weight gain? | Livestrong." Livestrong.com. Retrieved May 11, 2022.

Chertoff, J. (2019, February 26). "Muscular hypertrophy: The science and steps for building muscle." Healthline. Retrieved May 11, 2022.

Clayton, N., Drake, J., Larkin, S., Linkul, R., & Martino, M. (n.d.). "Foundations of fitness programming - NSCA." Foundations of fitness programming.

Gwin, J. A. (2018, May). The Effects of Dietary Protein at Breakfast and Across the Day on Appetite Control & Satiety, Food Intake, and Sleep Quality.

Helms, N. (2023, January 3). "Is the keto diet safe? what are the risks?". Is the Keto Diet Safe? What are the Risks? - UChicago Medicine.

How Bacteria Rule Over Your Body – The Microbiome. (2017). YouTube. Retrieved June 1, 2023.

Haff, G., & Triplett, N. T. (2021). "Essentials of strength training and conditioning" (4th ed.). Human Kinetics.

Jensen, M. (2017, August 21). "When women say they want to tone." Lean Bodies Consulting.

LIFEAID Beverage Co USA. (2022, September 7). "History of women's fitness." LIFEAID Beverage Co.

MediLexicon International. (n.d.). "Processed Foods: Health risks and what to avoid." Medical News Today. Retrieved June 16, 2022.

Pathak, D. (2018, August 16). "Muscle doesn't weigh more than fat." Baylor College of Medicine. Retrieved May 11, 2022.

Preiato, D. (2023, March 20). "5 side effects of pre-workout supplements." Healthline.

Reisinger, B. (2019, April 1). "The history of women in Fitness." IRONPLATE STUDIOS.

Rose, A. (2021b, May 18). "How (and why) to cycle your exercise with your menstrual cycle." Healthline.

Seal, A., Colburn, A., Johnson, E., Peronnet, F., Jansen, L., Adams, J., Bardis, C., Guelinckx, I., Perrier, E., & Kavouras9, S. (2022, August 9). Total water intake guidelines are sufficient for optimal hydration in United States adults. European journal of nutrition.

Solan, M. (2019, February 18). "The rise of push-ups: A classic exercise that can help you get stronger." Harvard Health. Retrieved June 21, 2022.

Stark, Matthew et al. "Protein timing and its effects on muscular hypertrophy and strength in individuals engaged in weight-training." Journal of the International Society of Sports Nutrition vol. 9,1 54. 14 Dec. 2012, doi:10.1186/1550-2783-9-54.

Suchomel, T., Nimphius, S., Bellon, C., & Stone, M. (2018). "The importance of muscular strength: Training considerations." Springer Nature.

Telegraph Media Group. (2014, January 7). "Women's wacky weight-loss regimes from the early 1920s and beyond." The Telegraph.

The importance of stretching. Harvard Health. (2022, March 14).

Therapeutic Associates Physical Therapy. (2021, May 18). "Myth: Lifting heavy weights will make me look bulky: Blog." Therapeutic Associates Physical Therapy. Retrieved May 15, 2022.

Valerio, R. (2019, May 3). "Fitness industry roundup: 'gym-timidation' is real." IHRSA. Retrieved May 14, 2022.

Weiss, L. W., et al. "Comparison of Serum Testosterone and Androstenedione Responses to Weight Lifting in Men and Women." European Journal of Applied Physiology and Occupational Physiology, vol. 50, no. 3, 1983, pp. 413–19, https://doiorg/10.1007/BF00423247.

World Health Organization. (n.d.). *Obesity and overweight*. World Health Organization.

Youngstedt, S. D., & Kline, C. E. (2006). Epidemiology of exercise and sleep. Sleep and biological rhythms, 4(3), 215–221.

ACKNOWLEDGEMENTS

When you are truly passionate and knowledgeable about a subject, a book comes naturally. I spent many late nights seated behind the glowing computer screen, desperately trying to type as fast as the thoughts and stories poured from my mind. The blue light reflected off my tired eyes, but I was too excited by the idea that this book would become a reality someday.

Despite this, writing a book, while also being a full-time biology student and personal trainer, took immense dedication and commitment. Every free second, my mind would wander back to this book and what I wanted to include within the pages. Even if I was riding the bus or on a run when a thought struck me, I would quickly open my iPhone to jot down notes. In a way, this book consumed my every thought for three years.

I have read countless books over the years, taking for granted the time and energy put into each one. However, after writing this book, I have a deeper understanding and true appreciation for the many hours and people it takes to make a dream a reality.

First and foremost, I'd like to thank my father, Rick Bright, whose insightful perspectives and honest feedback have been instrumental in shaping the content of this book. His wisdom and guidance have enriched its message, adding depth and clarity that would not have been possible without his contributions.

To my loving boyfriend, Michael, I extend my deepest gratitude for his support throughout the entire writing process. His belief in my abilities were a strong driving force behind my determination to see this project through. From offering soothing back rubs during moments of frustration to being my photographer for multiple photoshoots in order to get the cover *just* right, his presence has been a constant source of encouragement.

I extend my sincere thanks to my friend, Jacina Angelsberg, for her diligent efforts in providing grammar corrections and feedback. Her keen eye for detail and commitment to ensuring the accuracy and cohesiveness of the text improved the overall quality of this book.

I am also grateful to my supportive colleagues at work, Joanne, Alex, and Dr. Gentile, who graciously allowed me the freedom to work on this book during quieter periods in the office. Their understanding and encouragement have been instrumental in allowing me to balance my professional responsibilities with my passion for writing.

Last, but certainly not least, I express my appreciation to my mentors at Iconix Fitness, Ricardo, Adam, and Kurt. Their guidance, expertise, and belief in my potential played a pivotal role in shaping the trainer I am today. Their invaluable insights and wisdom have greatly influenced the content of this book, and I am grateful for their ongoing support.

Without the contributions and support of these incredible individuals, this book would have been a different and less exhilarating reality. Their presence has enriched the journey, infusing it with depth, passion, and a sense of community. I am forever grateful for their belief in me and their dedication to this project.

ABOUT THE AUTHOR

This is Nicki's first published book. Driven by her love for educating others and writing stories, she plans to write many more books in the future. Nicki is an online personal trainer and works in healthcare as a medical assistant. She lives in a tiny home with her boyfriend, Michael.

Follow Nicki on Instagram:

Nicki's Spotify workout playlist:

Made in the USA
Monee, IL
23 February 2025